## Praise for *A Light Still Burns*

"This book by an experienced and highly credentialed former military officer pungently and bravely advocates the case for Israel from personal experience and a perception of widespread antisemitism in this country. His heart and his head are passionately on display."

**—General the Honourable Sir Peter John Cosgrove AK AC (Mil) CVO MC (Ret.),** Governor-General of the Commonwealth of Australia, 2014–2019

"Sparked into action by the atrocities of October 7, Michael Scott brings his powerful perspective as a thirty-year veteran of the Australian army to combatting the dangerous and pernicious societal ill of antisemitism. You may not agree with his every critique how the political class, the media, and the United Nations have responded to this challenge, but after reading this book you will be left in no doubt about his indefatigable commitment to turning back this tide of hate. He understands rightly what it is at stake not just for Australia and Israel but for the wider world."

**—The Honourable Josh Frydenberg,** Treasurer of the Commonwealth of Australia, 2018–2022

"Colonel Michael Scott is a powerful and principled voice at a moment when clarity and courage are urgently needed. As a non-Jewish military leader with deep experience in the region, he brings rare moral authority to the defence of Israel and Western civilisation. His book, *A Light Still Burns*, is both timely and necessary—a clear-sighted contribution from a man who chooses to lead when it matters most."

**—Colonel Richard Kemp CBE (Ret.)**, former Commander of British Forces in Afghanistan

"Colonel Michael Scott offers a rare and powerful perspective in *A Light Still Burns*. Drawing on decades of outstanding military service and a deep personal journey, he sheds light on the moral clarity of Israel's struggle and the urgent need to stand against antisemitism. This book is both a timely warning and a call to conscience from an independent observer."

**—Colonel The Honourable Dr. Mike Kelly AM (Ret.)**, Former Australian Army Officer, Minister for Defence Materiel and Member for Eden Monaro. Adjunct Professor at the University of Canberra's National Security Institute

"Colonel Michael Scott has been a powerful voice in helping Australia and the international community understand the ongoing conflict in Israel and Gaza since October 7. As a decorated military officer with experience serving in Jerusalem, he brings a unique perspective to understanding the conflict."

—**Julian Leeser MP**, Federal Member for Berowra, Shadow Attorney-General

"*A Light Still Burns* is a clarion call from a warrior-scholar who understands the stakes of our time. Colonel Michael Scott brings the insight of lived experience and the conviction of a soldier unwilling to look away. This is not just a book about Israel—it is a defence of Western civilisation, moral courage, and the values worth standing up for. In an age of appeasement and ambiguity, Scott speaks with rare clarity and strength."

—**Major Andrew Fox (Ret.)**, British Army; Research Fellow, Henry Jackson Society

# A LIGHT STILL BURNS

## Israel and the Values Worth Defending

### MICHAEL SCOTT

A WICKED SON BOOK
An Imprint of Post Hill Press
ISBN: 979-8-89565-377-7
ISBN (eBook): 979-8-89565-378-4

A Light Still Burns:
Israel and the Values Worth Defending
© 2025 by Michael Scott
All Rights Reserved

Cover Design by Jim Villaflores

Post Hill Press
New York • Nashville
wickedsonbooks.com
posthillpress.com

Published in the United States of America
1  2  3  4  5  6  7  8  9  10

For Dracaena, Poppy, Charlie, Cameron, Georgina, and Ashton.

Mark Twain once said, "The two most important days in your life are the day you are born and the day you find out why." After October 7, 2023, I found my why. This book is part of my commitment to ensuring that future generations inherit a better world than the one we see today.

"I have believed passionately in the right of the State of Israel
to exist within secure and recognised boundaries. I have
believed in that right not just because of the horror of the
Holocaust but because the world should never have allowed
the Jewish people to be without a home and a refuge."

Bob Hawke
23rd Prime Minister of Australia


"A strong Israel is essential for a secure and just world."

John Howard
25th Prime Minister of Australia

# TABLE OF CONTENTS

# PREFACE

## BY MICHAEL SCOTT CSC

"In any moment of decision, the best thing you can do is the right thing, the next best thing is the wrong thing, and the worst thing you can do is nothing."

Theodore Roosevelt
26th President of the United States

Throughout history, civilisations have risen and fallen based on their ability to defend themselves—not just with swords and shields, but with ideas, principles, and moral clarity. Today, we find ourselves in an era where Western values, once considered unshakable, are being systematically undermined. The resurgence of antisemitism, the erosion of historical truth, and the rise of ideological movements that seek to dismantle the foundations of democracy and civilisation are all symptoms of this broader decline.

This book is a call to arms—not with weapons, but with words, facts, and unwavering moral conviction. It is a collection of essays that I have written since October 7, 2023, each grappling with the stark realities facing Israel, the Jewish people, and the broader Western world. Through these pages, I seek to expose the lies, challenge the false narratives, and provide a framework for understanding the existential battle in which we are engaged.

## WHY I WROTE THIS BOOK

I have spent three decades in the Australian Defence Force, serving in some of the world's most volatile regions. My experiences in Timor-Leste, Bougainville, Iraq, and Afghanistan have given me a deep appreciation for the complexities of war, peace, and national survival. However, nothing shaped my worldview more profoundly than the years I spent in Israel.

From July 2019 to September 2021, I lived in Jerusalem while seconded to a United Nations peacekeeping mission. My role required me to travel extensively across the region—Israel, Lebanon, Syria, Jordan, and Egypt—engaging with military, diplomatic, and non-government officials together with citizens of the Levant. I witnessed firsthand the challenges Israel faces: the relentless existential threats from terrorist organisations, the moral dilemmas of asymmetrical warfare, and the absurd double standards imposed by the international community.

Yet, what struck me most was not just Israel's capacity for self-defence, but its resilience, ingenuity, and profound sense of humanity. It is a nation that has not only survived against all odds but has thrived, despite unrelenting hostility. It is a people who have turned deserts into gardens, persecution into perseverance, and adversity into strength.

In the aftermath of that atrocious display at the Sydney Opera House on October 9, 2023, I resolved to not be a bystander. To combat antisemitism, defend Israel's rightful place in the world, and fight for the preservation of Western civilisation. In July 2024, I founded The 2023 Foundation Ltd with my wife, Dracaena, to take this calling beyond words and into action. This book is part of that mission.

## THE BATTLE FOR TRUTH

Israel's struggle is not just military—it is informational, ideological, and existential. The war against the Jewish state is fought not only with rockets and terrorism but with lies, propaganda, and historical revisionism. The modern battlefield is as much in university lecture halls, media outlets, and on social media platforms as it is in the streets of Gaza or the hills of Judea and Samaria.

We live in an age where truth itself is under siege. The events of October 7, 2023, when Hamas terrorists launched the deadliest attack on Israel in decades, were a horrifying wake-up call. The massacre of innocent civilians, the widespread use of rape as a weapon of war, and the sadistic slaughter of entire families were met with a chilling response—not just from Hamas's apologists in the Arab world, but from left-wing activists, academics, and even Western governments who refused to unequivocally condemn the atrocities. Instead, they sought to "contextualise" the bloodshed, to justify the unjustifiable, and to place blame not on the perpetrators but on the victims.

This pattern is not new. The world has long been comfortable with Jewish suffering but intolerant of Jewish strength. When Jews are persecuted, the world issues solemn declarations of remembrance. When Jews fight back, they are called oppressors. This hypocrisy must be exposed and challenged.

This book is my contribution to that effort. It is a defence of Israel's right to exist—not merely as a political entity but as a moral necessity. It is a rejection of the poisonous ideologies that seek to erode Western civilisation from within. It is a challenge to the complacency, cowardice, and intellectual dishonesty that allow antisemitism to fester unchecked.

## WHAT THIS BOOK OFFERS

This book is structured into thematic sections, each addressing a critical aspect of the struggle for truth and civilisation.

- **Section I – The Eternal Struggle:** Examines the persistence of antisemitism, from historical pogroms to its modern resurgence in the West, exposing how hatred of the Jewish people evolves yet never truly disappears.
- **Section II – The Iron Shield:** Explores Israel's security challenges, the ethical dilemmas of warfare, and the double standards imposed on the Jewish state, revealing how Israel is condemned for doing what any other nation would consider self-preservation.
- **Section III – The War of Perception:** Dissects how misinformation, media bias, and academic corruption fuel the delegitimisation of Israel and Western values, turning propaganda into mainstream discourse.
- **Section IV – The West at a Crossroads:** Situates Israel's struggle within the larger decline of Western civilisation, warning against moral relativism, ideological subversion, and the erosion of democratic societies.
- **Section V – Winning the Peace:** Offers a strategic roadmap for Israel and its allies, outlining what must change in policy, diplomacy, and global engagement to secure a just and lasting future.

Each essay is framed within a broader narrative, providing historical context, strategic analysis, and firsthand insight to help readers connect the dots between seemingly disparate events. Together, they form a mosaic of the ideological battle being waged today—one that will shape the future of our world.

## WHO THIS BOOK IS FOR

This book is for those who refuse to be bystanders. It is for those who understand that silence in the face of evil is complicity. It is for Jews and non-Jews alike who recognise that the fight against antisemitism is not merely about protecting one people—it is about defending the values that uphold free societies.

It is for those who are tired of media distortions, historical amnesia, and intellectual cowardice. It is for those who seek clarity in an age of deliberate confusion. It is for those who refuse to accept the false equivalence between democracy and terrorism, between civilisation and barbarism.

And above all, it is for those who understand that the battle for Israel's survival is inseparable from the battle for the survival of Western civilisation itself.

## A FINAL THOUGHT

In one of his final speeches, Winston Churchill warned that the greatest threat to civilisation was not external aggression but internal decay. "To each there comes in their lifetime a special moment when they are figuratively tapped on the shoulder and offered the chance to do a very special thing, unique to them and fitted to their talents," he said. "What a tragedy if that moment finds them unprepared or unqualified for that which could have been their finest hour."

I have felt the tap on my shoulder. This book is my response.

The battle is far from over, but we are not powerless. We can push back against the tide. We can expose the lies. We can challenge the distortions. We can defend truth, justice, and civilisation itself. We have agency and ought to use it.

That is the mission of this book.

**Together, we will prevail.** חצנב דחי

# THE ETERNAL STRUGGLE – ANTISEMITISM AND ITS MODERN RESURGENCE

## INTRODUCTION TO SECTION I

Antisemitism is often referred to as the world's oldest hatred, but that label risks making it seem like an archaic relic of history rather than an ever-present threat. It is not confined to the past—it is alive and thriving in today's world, rebranded, repackaged, and repurposed to suit the ideological, political, and social currents of our time.

The events of October 7, 2023, when Hamas massacred Israeli civilians in an act of unfathomable brutality, should have shattered any illusions about Israel's security and the safety of its people. But instead of universal condemnation, Western elites found ways to justify the bloodshed. They excused Hamas, blamed Israel, and in doing so, revealed how deeply antisemitism has embedded itself within the modern world.

This section explores the various manifestations of antisemitism in contemporary society. Some are overt and violent, like the attacks on Jewish communities and institutions worldwide. Others are subtler but equally corrosive, emerging in academia, journalism, and progressive politics under the guise of "anti-Zionism." Each essay in this section contributes to a broader picture of a world that has, yet again, become comfortable with Jewish suffering.

The past year has demonstrated a chilling reality: We are witnessing a historical repetition. The pogroms of past centuries have returned, just in a modern form. The question, then, is this: Will we have the courage to fight back before history completes the rhyme?

# THE RECURRING NIGHTMARE: ANTISEMITISM THROUGH THE AGES

## INTRODUCTION

The term "pogrom" originates from the Russian Empire, where violent massacres against Jewish communities were often tolerated or even encouraged by local authorities. These attacks, marked by looting, murder, and mass displacement, were a defining feature of European antisemitism in the nineteenth and early twentieth centuries.

Many assume pogroms are a relic of history. They are not. The October 7, 2023, massacre in Israel was a modern pogrom—an organised, ideologically motivated slaughter of Jews. But what made it even more chilling was the reaction. Instead of universal condemnation, the attacks were met with justifications, denials, and even celebrations in parts of the West.

This essay examines how the patterns of historical pogroms are repeating today—not just through violent attacks but through the ideological acceptance of Jewish victimisation. It challenges the notion that these horrors are confined to the past and exposes how modern antisemitism fuels the same cycle of persecution.

## POGROM

*First published in The Australian Jewish News, March 28, 2025*

The word "pogrom" evokes fear and trauma, particularly within Jewish communities, symbolising violent persecution and historical suffering. Reflecting on Ronald Lauder's powerful remarks at the 80th commemoration of the liberation of Auschwitz and Birkenau, we are reminded that remembrance alone is not enough—it must be accompanied by decisive action. As Lauder poignantly stated: "The extermination of the Jews in World War II was a step-by-step process aided by those who hated Jews, but advanced by the indifference of people who thought they were not affected because they were not Jewish."

Lauder, a philanthropist and president of the World Jewish Congress, has been a prominent advocate for Holocaust remembrance and the fight against antisemitism. His recent remarks highlighted that the past cannot merely be remembered—it requires active engagement. Citing Elie Wiesel's observation that "the opposite of love is not hate, but indifference," Lauder urged governments, educators, and civil society to address the resurgence of hatred. He cautioned that silence in the face of injustice fuels its spread and emphasised that "education is the most effective tool in dismantling hate."

Drawing parallels between the pre-Holocaust era and today's rising antisemitism, Lauder stated, "It was the world's silence that led to Auschwitz." He noted with concern that "Jewish children are being told to hide outward signs of being Jewish," evoking disturbing echoes of the past. His call to action is clear: "Let today be the day all of us make a pledge—not to be silent when it comes to antisemitism."

Under Lauder's leadership, the World Jewish Congress has championed Holocaust remembrance, supported Jewish communities globally, and tackled modern antisemitism. His unwavering commitment provides a beacon of hope that through education and collective action, we can create a more tolerant and inclusive world. "The lessons of Auschwitz," Lauder reminds us, "are not just about the past—they are about the future."

## Understanding Pogroms — Definition and Characteristics

A pogrom refers to an organised massacre or violent attack against a specific group, most notably Jews, though the term has broader applications. It derives from the Russian *pogrom*, meaning "to destroy" or "to wreak havoc." Historically, pogroms were often state-sanctioned or tolerated by local authorities, resulting in widespread violence, destruction, and displacement.

Key characteristics of pogroms include the following:

- **Violence and Looting:** Mass killings, physical assaults, sexual violence, and the destruction of homes, synagogues, and businesses
- **State Complicity:** Passive inaction or active encouragement by authorities in the violence
- **Forced Displacement:** Loss of homes, possessions, and communities

## A Historical Perspective: The Kishinev Pogrom (1903)

One of the most infamous pogroms occurred in Kishinev (now Chisinau, Moldova) in 1903. Over two days, forty-nine Jews were murdered, hundreds were injured, and countless homes and businesses were destroyed. The violence was triggered by a false accusation—a blood libel claiming that Jews had murdered a Christian boy for ritual purposes—and fuelled by antisemitic propaganda.

The authorities' complicity made the massacre particularly devastating. Police stood by, offering no protection to the Jewish community. While the international outcry condemned the violence, it did little to prevent future pogroms across Eastern Europe and Russia.

## Beyond the Russian Empire: Pogroms Across History

While most associated with the Russian Empire's persecution of Jews, pogrom-like violence has occurred throughout history against various minority groups. Examples include the following:

- The anti-Armenian massacres in the late Ottoman Empire
- The anti-Catholic Gordon Riots in eighteenth-century London
- Kristallnacht (1938), a state-sponsored pogrom in Nazi Germany

The defining feature of a pogrom is its organised nature, often with explicit or implicit state approval. Pogroms signal societal decay, where prejudice and bigotry are left to fester and escalate.

## Pogroms and Antisemitic Violence in the Last Fifty Years

Antisemitic violence has persisted globally, manifesting in large-scale attacks and systematic persecution. Below is a summary of key events that mirror historical pogroms:

### State-Sanctioned Persecution and Exodus

- **Iran (Post-1979):** Following the Islamic Revolution, Iran's Jewish population faced persecution, forcing mass emigration. Public executions of Jewish leaders, including Habib Elghanian, sent shockwaves through the community.
- **Soviet Union (1970s–1980s):** Jews faced discrimination, surveillance, and imprisonment. International pressure eventually enabled hundreds of thousands to emigrate to Israel and the United States.
- **Argentina (1976–1983):** During the military dictatorship, roughly 3,000 Jews were among the 30,000 who disappeared.
- **Lebanon (1975–1990):** Pogrom-like violence and assassinations of Jewish leaders forced most of the community to flee.
- **Syria (1970s–1990s):** Harassment and surveillance led to mass emigration, culminating in the lifting of travel bans in 1992.
- **Ethiopia (1984–1991):** Operations Moses and Solomon airlifted thousands of Ethiopian Jews to Israel, helping them escape persecution.

- **Yemen (1990s–2010s):** Abductions, forced conversions, and harassment led to the near-total disappearance of Yemen's Jewish community.

## *Modern Pogrom-Like Incidents*

- **Crown Heights Riots (1991, US):** Violent riots targeted Orthodox Jews in Brooklyn, resulting in multiple injuries and the murder of Yankel Rosenbaum.
- **France (2000s–Present):** Rising antisemitic violence, including the 2015 Hypercacher kosher supermarket attack, has driven many French Jews to emigrate.
- **Pittsburgh Synagogue Shooting (2018, US):** The deadliest antisemitic attack in US history left eleven worshippers dead.
- **October 7, 2023 (Israel):** Hamas launched an unprecedented attack on Israel, murdering over 1,200 people and taking hostages. It is described as one of the deadliest antisemitic assaults since the Holocaust.
- **November 7, 2024 (Amsterdam):** Organised violence targeted Israeli football fans, highlighting rising antisemitism in Europe.

These incidents underscore the ongoing vulnerability of Jewish communities worldwide. Many Jews have sought refuge in Israel, reinforcing its role as a haven. However, combating antisemitism requires global cooperation, education, and proactive action.

## Why Ronald Lauder's Speech Matters

During his Auschwitz speech, Lauder underscored the urgent need for education to combat antisemitism:

*"Education is the most powerful tool we have to combat hate. If we fail to educate, we leave the door open for history to repeat itself."*

## The Role of Education

Effective education must go beyond historical recollection—it must foster critical thinking, social responsibility, and proactive engagement. Strategies include the following:

- **Holocaust and Genocide Studies:** Schools should teach the causes and consequences of mass violence.
- **Critical Thinking and Media Literacy:** Young people must learn to recognise propaganda and misinformation.
- **Community Engagement:** Local initiatives can promote tolerance and understanding.
- **Survivor Testimonies:** Personal stories humanise history, making denial harder.
- **Addressing Modern Prejudices:** Lessons must connect past and present forms of hatred.

## Conclusion: Together, We Will Prevail

Ronald Lauder's message is a call to action. The fight against antisemitism is ongoing, but through education, advocacy, and collective vigilance, we can push back against hatred.

The word "pogrom" should belong to history—not the present. Whether it remains a relic of the past or resurfaces in our time depends on the choices we make as a society. It is our actions—or our inaction—that will determine the course of history.

I, for one, refuse to be a bystander.

# 2

# HOW WE FORGOT TO SEE THE ENEMY

## INTRODUCTION

Western societies have grown obsessed with "safety"—but only in selective ways. We censor speech, monitor words, and enforce political correctness, yet we fail to recognise or confront real dangers. We treat ideological extremism as an abstract academic debate rather than an existential threat.

The October 7 attacks were a brutal reminder of what happens when societies lose their ability to distinguish between genuine threats and imagined ones. Hamas's ideology was clear. Their intent was clear. Yet, many in the West, blinded by ideological naivety, refused to see it coming. Even after the attacks, there was widespread hesitation to acknowledge the scale of brutality. This failure is not unique to Israel—it is part of a broader Western pattern of self-delusion when dealing with Islamist extremism.

This essay explores the consequences of ignoring warning signs, the erosion of Western vigilance, and the lethal cost of losing our instinct for danger.

# LOSING OUR INSTINCT FOR DANGER

*First published in The Australian Jewish News, March 26, 2025*

The world is once again confronted with a horrifying reminder of what happens when we ignore the obvious: the brutal murder of the Bibas family in Gaza. The tragic fate of this beautiful young family, whose images have haunted our collective conscience since October 7, is not an aberration—it is a direct consequence of Gaza's radicalisation and the global reluctance to acknowledge this reality.

For decades, the international community has chosen to believe in the illusion that a meaningful distinction exists between civilians and combatants in Gaza. The truth, however, is starkly different and becoming increasingly problematic to deny. Hamas does not merely govern Gaza—it is Gaza. The indoctrination, the glorification of martyrdom, and the eradication of dissenting voices have ensured that radical jihadist ideology is not just prevalent but fundamental to life in Gaza. This radicalisation is not merely political; it is deeply rooted in Jew-hatred, a core pillar of Hamas's doctrine.

## A Firsthand Account of Radicalisation

In a poignant reflection on her harrowing experience, Mia Schem, a 21-year-old French Israeli woman abducted during the October 7, 2023, Nova music festival massacre, shared chilling insights into the pervasive indoctrination within Gaza. After enduring fifty-four days of captivity, Schem recounted being held in a confined space, often taunted by young children who, despite their tender ages, exhibited deep-seated animosity. She observed that even the youngest members of Gazan society are inculcated with extremist ideologies, leading her to conclude, "Everyone there are terrorists... there are no innocent civilians, not one."

Initially, Schem's statements upon release suggested she was treated with care; however, she later clarified that these remarks were coerced by her captors for propaganda purposes. Her subsequent accounts underscore the psychological manipulation and the extent of radicalisation present, even among children in Gaza. Schem's experiences highlight the profound challenges in distinguishing between combatants and non-combatants in such an environment, raising critical questions about the societal structures that perpetuate such pervasive hostility and Jew-hatred.

I was initially sceptical upon hearing Schem's accounts. However, as days turned into months and now years, with no signs of moderation or softening of radical Islam in Gaza—or within Australia's local Muslim community, for that matter—I find myself re-evaluating my earlier perspective.

## Without Precedent: The Radicalisation of an Entire Society

Throughout history, barbarian hordes have threatened the survival of civilisations—whether it was the Vandals sacking Rome, the Huns sweeping across Europe, or the Visigoths dismantling the remnants of classical antiquity. These peoples, often painted as ruthless invaders, wielded brutality as a weapon, yet their violence was driven by conquest, not by an ideology that consumed their entire societies from infancy to adulthood. The thorough radicalisation of the Gazan population, including its youth, has no clear historical parallel.

Unlike past barbarian tribes, who waged war to gain territory and resources, Gaza's radicalisation is ideological, absolute, and multi-generational. This transformation has not occurred through the natural ebb and flow of tribal warfare but has been accelerated by the modern information age—an era in which propaganda spreads faster than armies ever could. Put simply, we have enabled this by incentivising and rewarding bad behaviour. It is an uncomfortable truth that the West must confront; we have played a direct role in cultivating this extremism.

Through decades of funding institutions like the United Nations Relief and Works Agency (UNRWA), Western taxpayers have unknowingly financed the indoctrination of an entire generation, ensuring that hatred—especially Jew-hatred—is not merely sustained but deeply institutionalised. From Gazan kindergartens teaching martyrdom to West Bank clerics preaching genocidal rhetoric, the extremism we now face is, in part, a product of our own misguided benevolence. This is not just a regional crisis; it is a stark warning of what happens when societies unwittingly finance their own destruction.

## International Humanitarian Law and the Radicalisation of Gaza

International law is clear about what transforms a civilian into a combatant. Under the Geneva Conventions, civilians lose their protected status when they take direct part in hostilities. But what constitutes direct participation? Does it extend to those who aid combatants before or after an attack? What about those who take or imprison hostages, serve as lookouts, or facilitate military operations? The legal consensus is that individuals who knowingly contribute to the war effort—whether by transporting fighters, relaying intelligence, supplying weapons, or providing logistical support—may forfeit civilian protections.

Likewise, when a mosque, school, or UN facility is repurposed to store weapons, coordinate attacks, or shelter combatants, it ceases to be a protected site and becomes a legitimate military target under international law. The presence of civilians, including children, in such locations does not automatically reinstate their protected status if the site is actively used for military purposes. These principles reinforce that the true responsibility for endangering civilian lives lies not with those enforcing the laws of war but with those who systematically violate them by embedding their forces among non-combatants, using human shields, and weaponising civilian infrastructure.

The principle of proportionality dictates that military responses must not inflict excessive harm relative to the military advantage gained. Legal scholar Natasha Hausdorff emphasises, "Proportionality does not mean an equal response; it requires that the force used is necessary and not excessive in relation to the concrete and direct military advantage anticipated."

## The Radicalisation of Gaza is Total

The murder of the Bibas family compels us to ask: What does it say about a society when such horrors are not condemned but celebrated? What does it mean when a population cheers the abduction of children?

Douglas Murray, one of the most lucid commentators of our time, has long warned against the West's naive engagement with radical Islamists. "The problem," he states, "is not just the people with guns and bombs, but the ideology that supports them."

Andrew Fox, a former British military officer, echoes this concern. "We have been conditioned to second-guess ourselves, to silence our gut reactions in the name of tolerance and diversity," Fox observes. But misplaced tolerance has lethal consequences.

## The West Must Regain Its Instinct for Danger

The survival of Western civilisation depends on our ability to recognise and confront threats as they truly are, not as we wish them to be. The murder of the Bibas family is not just another tragedy—it is a warning. If we continue to suppress our instinct for self-preservation, we will condemn ourselves to a future far darker than we dare imagine.

The time for illusions is over.

# 3

# WHEN HATRED TAKES TO THE STREETS

## INTRODUCTION

On December 4, 2024, a mob surrounded The Great Synagogue in Sydney during an academic event celebrating Israel's technological contributions. Inside, Jewish and non-Jewish leaders gathered to discuss medical advancements and humanitarian progress. Outside, a frenzied crowd chanted hatred, threats, and calls for Jewish blood.

This moment was a reminder that mob violence against Jews is not a thing of the past—it is alive today, in Western capitals, fuelled by ideological fervour and political cowardice.

This essay examines the historical and contemporary phenomenon of antisemitic mobs, how political leaders are failing to confront them, and what must be done before another tragedy strikes.

## THE BAYING MOB – WHEN AND HOW DOES THIS END?

*First published in The Australian Jewish News, December 6, 2024*

On the evening of December 4, 2024, I joined a distinguished group of Jewish and non-Jewish philanthropists at The Great Synagogue in Sydney's Central Business District to commemorate the one hundredth anniversary of the Technion–Israel Institute of Technology. The event was a testament to the boundless potential of human ingenuity and cooperation. It began with a powerful "Welcome to Country" by Nova Peris, followed by the singing of the Australian National Anthem. Esteemed presenters, including visiting professors and alumni, showcased groundbreaking work in medical research and other disciplines—innovations poised to benefit people of all backgrounds, irrespective of race, religion, or political affiliation. It was a living embodiment of Tikkun Olam, a Hebrew term meaning "repairing the world."

Inside the synagogue, there was a palpable sense of peace, tolerance, and a celebration of life (chai). Yet, outside its walls, the atmosphere was one of hostility and hatred. A baying mob gathered, their chants and placards reflecting visceral anger devoid of reason or humanity. From a distance, they appeared to be a mix of Anglo zealots and misguided activists. Their presence demonstrated that one can pass through the finest schools and universities, yet remain bereft of any meaningful education about history, empathy, or decency.

Sitting within the synagogue, I couldn't shake a profound unease—a gnawing sense that history was echoing in the present. It was not lost on me that Jewish communities have faced similar threats throughout history. In centuries past, synagogues besieged by mobs were set ablaze, trapping those inside to die by fire or suffocation. These horrors are not confined to the distant past; they are etched into the collective memory of Jewish communities across the world.

## Is This How It Ends?

Will it take a tragedy akin to the murder of British soldier Lee Rigby, butchered on the streets of London in 2013, for Australia's elected officials to comprehend the gravity of the times in which we live? The mob outside The Great Synagogue that night bore no weapons, but their actions and rhetoric were steeped in the kind of hatred that historically precedes unspeakable violence.

I consider myself well-read, and through my years of study, I have come to appreciate the predictive power of history. As Mark Twain is often credited with observing, "History doesn't repeat itself, but it often rhymes." Nowhere in recorded history can I find an example of antisemitism, such as that seen in 1930s Europe or today's manifestations, resolving itself through inaction. On the contrary, history shows that these movements escalate until confronted by collective moral courage. To borrow Edmund Burke's timeless wisdom: "The only thing necessary for the triumph of evil is for good men to do nothing."

The question, then, is this: When will enough good men and women stand up and say, "Stop!"?

This is not a call for vigilante justice but a plea for our elected officials—state and federal—to rise to the occasion and enact meaningful measures to ensure the safety and dignity of all citizens. While I have great respect for Australia's law enforcement agencies, I recognise that in our democracy, the ultimate responsibility rests with those we elect to lead us.

The time for rhetoric has long passed. Action is needed. Facta non verba—deeds, not words. If this baying mob is allowed to persist unchecked, it is only a matter of time before we face a tragedy. Whether it be an individual decapitated in an Australian suburb or citizens burnt alive in places of worship, history has shown us the consequences of ignoring the warning signs.

As a thirty-year veteran of the Australian Army with combat experience, I do not raise these concerns lightly. Writing this piece is not an act of alarmism but one of deep concern, borne of a lifetime of service to this nation and its ideals. That such a piece feels necessary should signal to all that we are failing at a fundamental level—and that failure must be addressed with urgency and resolve.

Enough is enough.

Let us learn from history, not repeat its darkest chapters. Let us repair our nation's moral compass and act decisively to ensure that tolerance, dignity, and peace prevail. Let us ensure that the future we build is one we can all be proud of.

4

# CUTTING THROUGH THE PROPAGANDA

## INTRODUCTION

The war against Israel is not just military—it is a war of perception. In the digital age, antisemitism spreads through misinformation, propaganda, and deliberate deception. Israel is demonised not because of what it does, but because of what it represents: strength, survival, and the refusal to be victimised.

The lies are insidious. Terrorists are called "freedom fighters." The world's only Jewish state is labelled a "colonial project," ignoring 3,000 years of Jewish history in the land. Israel's defence against terror is framed as aggression, while actual aggression against Israelis is excused or ignored.

This essay exposes the mechanisms of deception used against Israel and the Jewish people. It reveals how misinformation spreads, who benefits from it, and why the truth is often buried under layers of ideological distortion.

# SEEING THROUGH THE LIES, ARTIFICE, AND DECEPTION

*First published in The Australian Jewish News, March 25, 2025*

Lies, artifice, and deception—tools as old as human interaction—have shaped decisions and perceptions throughout history, and they remain disturbingly relevant today. In a quote often attributed to Mark Twain, it is aptly observed that "A lie can travel halfway around the world while the truth is putting on its shoes." From the alarming resurgence of antisemitism to the erosion of Judeo-Christian values that have long underpinned Western democracies, the world faces a multifaceted ideological assault. These two trends are deeply interlinked, each reinforcing the other to weaken societal cohesion. They erode the moral framework that has upheld principles of justice, individual rights, and human dignity, leaving Western societies increasingly vulnerable to division and manipulation.

## Antisemitism and Public Opinion

One of the most troubling aspects of this phenomenon is how deception targets not only governments and institutions but also public opinion. Antisemitism is a prime example, with recent data from the Anti-Defamation League (ADL) revealing that nearly half of the global population harbours antisemitic views. Alarmingly, these attitudes are not shaped by personal experience or direct interaction but are instead informed by twisted narratives and opinion, perpetuated through lies, propaganda, and misinformation. Social media has amplified these falsehoods, allowing hateful ideologies to spread at unprecedented speeds and contributing to deepening societal divisions.

The ADL's 2025 report, released on 16 January 2025, highlighted a concerning rise in antisemitic sentiment worldwide. Among its findings, 46 percent of respondents across surveyed nations admitted to holding antisemitic views—a significant increase from previous years. Even more troubling, 21 percent believed the Holocaust was exaggerated or fabricated, and 20 percent admitted they had never heard of it. These figures underscore the scale of ignorance and the potency of misinformation in shaping public opinion. Recent surveys also indicate a worrying generational trend: Younger cohorts, inundated with social media misinformation, are more susceptible to adopting distorted views.

## Adverse Influencers in the West

In recent years, several major Western media outlets in Australia, the United States, and the United Kingdom have faced accusations of disseminating antisemitic messages or exhibiting bias in their reporting on Jewish-related issues. Notable examples include

- **Australia – Australian Broadcasting Corporation (ABC):** The ABC has faced criticism for providing platforms that may inadvertently amplify antisemitic sentiments. Discussions on the rise of antisemitism have pointed to the role of media in spreading hate speech, with the ABC being urged to exercise caution in its reporting to avoid contributing to such issues.
- **United States – MSNBC:** The network has faced criticism for its coverage of events related to Israel and Jewish communities. During a segment on the attacks in Israel, Anti-Defamation League CEO Jonathan

Greenblatt appeared on MSNBC's *Morning Joe* to critique the network's depiction of Hamas and the conflict, urging for accurate terminology and reporting.

- **United Kingdom – British Broadcasting Corporation (BBC):** The BBC has been criticised by Jewish community leaders for perceived institutional hostility towards Israel. A report by former BBC executives Danny Cohen and Ruth Deech highlighted concerns about the broadcaster's impartiality, suggesting that its reporting fuels antisemitism and undermines the security of Jewish communities. The BBC has faced calls for an independent inquiry into these allegations.

## Weaponising Lies, Artifice, and Deception

Deceptive tactics employed by state and non-state actors exploit Western values and cultural blind spots. The following case studies illustrate the scope of this challenge:

- **The Gaza Hospital Narrative:** On 17 October 2023, an explosion at the Al-Ahli Arab Hospital in Gaza was immediately attributed to an Israeli airstrike by Hamas, claiming 500 fatalities. Media outlets amplified this narrative without verification, sparking global outrage. Subsequent investigations revealed that a misfired Palestinian Islamic Jihad rocket caused the explosion, with casualties far fewer than initially reported. This incident underscores how rapid misinformation, coupled with media bias, can inflame tensions and shape global opinion.

- **Hezbollah's "Green Without Borders":** Ostensibly an environmental conservation group, Hezbollah's "Green

Without Borders" serves as a front for military operations along the Israeli-Lebanese border. Under the guise of ecological projects, it facilitates surveillance and logistical support for hostilities against Israel.

- **Russia's Maskirovka:** Russia's strategic deception, or maskirovka (маскировка), combines misinformation, psychological manipulation, and camouflage. From its historical use in World War II to its modern application during the 2014 annexation of Crimea, maskirovka blurs truth and fiction, delaying international responses.

- **China's Salami-Slicing Tactics:** Drawing on Sun Tzu's *The Art of War*, China employs incremental actions—such as building artificial islands in the South China Sea—that appear benign individually but collectively advance its territorial claims.

## The Work of The 2023 Foundation

As someone who lived in Israel while on a military secondment with a United Nations Peacekeeping Mission, I have witnessed firsthand the stark contrast between lived experience and the narratives perpetuated by biased media or ideological zealots. My time in Israel revealed a nation defined by both its challenges and its remarkable achievements—a place of "perfect imperfection" that defies simplistic stereotypes.

A love of Israel cannot be taught; it must be caught. You cannot understand and appreciate the nuance or see how reality is so different from what is portrayed on the ABC or in the cesspit of social media unless you travel to Israel and experience it for yourself.

The 2023 Foundation was established to bridge this gap, offering opportunities for reasonable, open-minded individuals to engage directly with Israel and its people. By fostering personal experiences, we aim to counter misinformation and challenge the distorted narratives that fuel antisemitism. Our website, www.2023foundation.org.au, highlights how direct exposure fosters understanding and empathy, combating deception with authenticity.

## Conclusion

We live in an uneasy calm—a precarious age where deception, propaganda, and division erode the cohesion of Western democracies. As Thomas Jefferson wisely warned, "The price of freedom is eternal vigilance." This timeless reminder underscores the critical need to recognise and confront lies, artifice, and deception before they further undermine the values that sustain our societies.

Antisemitism stands as a stark cautionary example, reflecting the corrosive power of misinformation and the widespread misperceptions about Israel perpetuated by distorted narratives. While the Jewish community holds agency in addressing these challenges, Israel's primary responsibility—and focus—must remain on securing its survival in an existential struggle.

Yet, this is not a task for Israel alone. Jewish diaspora communities, along with gentiles—like me—who understand the truth about Israel, must rise to the challenge. It is my judgement that we may be losing the "silent majority." While our gaze was elsewhere, antisemites and ideological malcontents worked feverishly, embedding their falsehoods and sowing division. We are now in a race to catch up. This competition for hearts and minds is one we cannot afford to lose. Global demographic trends, coupled with the generational erosion of support for Israel, magnify the urgency of our mission. The stakes are too high for passivity; decisive action is essential to reclaim and fortify the foundational support required for Israel's enduring survival.

A steadfast commitment to truth, vigilance, and collaborative action is not merely desirable—it is indispensable. Only with such resolve can we preserve the principles and values that underpin democratic societies and secure a future where justice, integrity, and coexistence prevail.

5

# CASUAL HATRED: WHEN PREJUDICE HIDES BEHIND IGNORANCE

## INTRODUCTION

Some of the most dangerous forms of antisemitism do not come from swastika-waving extremists but from ignorant, well-meaning individuals who think they are standing for justice. They chant "from the river to the sea" without understanding its genocidal implications. They parrot media narratives without questioning their source. They vote for policies that undermine Jewish security, all while believing they are acting morally.

This essay confronts the rise of "unconscious antisemites"—those who fuel antisemitism not out of malice, but out of ignorance, naivety, or ideological indoctrination.

## THE UNCONSCIOUS ANTISEMITE: IGNORANCE IS NO EXCUSE

*First published in The Australian Jewish News, December 18, 2024*

I agree with Douglas Murray's observation: There exists a motley cabal of antisemites who span a range from the sinister to the silly. The sinister are those who chant genocidal slogans about freeing Palestine "from the river to the sea" with full awareness of their implications. The silly, on the other hand, often have no clue about the geography they reference, let alone the complex history of the conflict. Caught up in ideology, social trends, or plain ignorance, these individuals may not even grasp the toxicity of their positions.

If you find your opinions on Israel shaped predominantly by selective programming from the Australian Broadcasting Corporation (ABC) or the fevered takes of social media, you may have been misled. A strange coalition of Islamists, anarchists, Marxists, and hard-left zealots has coalesced around the banner of anti-Zionism, forming what historians may one day regard as one of the oddest alliances in history. But it is not enough to dismiss this movement as "silly" or ideologically confused—it is a significant driver of the rising antisemitism we see today.

## The "Unconscious Antisemite"

In contemporary Australia, a subtle yet pervasive form of antisemitism has emerged, often masquerading as legitimate criticism of Israel. This phenomenon, which I term the "unconscious antisemite," involves individuals who, perhaps unwittingly, perpetuate age-old prejudices under the guise of political discourse. These are people who might not identify as antisemitic and may even abhor racism in other forms, yet their actions and words serve to marginalise Jewish communities and delegitimise Jewish self-determination.

Anti-Zionism—the denial of the Jewish people's right to self-determination—is not a neutral political stance; it is inherently antisemitic. The International Holocaust Remembrance

Alliance (IHRA) defines antisemitism as "a certain perception of Jews, which may be expressed as hatred toward Jews." This includes actions that target Jewish individuals, communities, or institutions, as well as those that demonise Israel or apply double standards to the Jewish state.

## Sharansky's 3D Test

Natan Sharansky's "3D Test" offers further clarity, identifying three key components of antisemitism disguised as criticism of Israel:

- **Delegitimisation:** Denying Israel's fundamental right to exist
- **Demonisation:** Portraying Israel and its people as inherently evil
- **Double Standards:** Holding Israel to scrutiny and moral expectations not applied to any other nation

These criteria illuminate how contemporary antisemitism often cloaks itself in political rhetoric, making it vital to identify and confront it wherever it appears.

## Insights from the Munk Debate

The recent Munk Debate underscored these points. Natasha Hausdorff, an international law expert, observed: "Anti-Zionism singles out Jewish self-determination for scorn, making it an unmistakable form of antisemitism." Journalist and author Douglas Murray added: "Those who say that the Jewish state alone is illegitimate are not simply anti-Zionist but antisemitic and bear responsibility for rising hate crimes against Jews worldwide." These insights highlight the intrinsic bias and danger of anti-Zionism as a political stance.

## The Curious Coalition Against Zionism

Adding to this complexity is the paradoxical coalition of support and opposition around Zionism. Various ethnic and religious groups—such as Iranians, Lebanese Maronite and Orthodox Christians, Coptic Christians, Druze, and Kurds—often express strong support for Zionism. These communities, familiar with historical oppression and the fight for self-determination, resonate with the Jewish narrative and see Israel as a model of resilience and democracy.

In stark contrast, some Anglo-Australians, influenced by a cocktail of ideological trends and moral relativism, exhibit passive or active antisemitism. At best, they are "unconscious"; at worst, they are just bigots in denial. This inconsistency raises serious questions about the values and awareness within certain segments of our society. How can those who champion progressive causes turn a blind eye—or worse, lend their voices—to rhetoric that marginalises and endangers an entire community?

## Judeo-Christian Values and the Erosion of Solidarity

Judeo-Christian values have long underpinned Western civilisation, emphasising justice, equality, and the sanctity of human life. These principles should naturally foster solidarity with Jewish communities and Israel. Yet, the rise of cultural relativism and distorted moral frameworks has eroded these values, replacing them with a corrosive ideology that excuses or even endorses prejudice.

This distortion must be called out for what it is. Standing against antisemitism is not simply about protecting one community—it is about upholding the values that bind our society together.

## A Call to Action

Australia is not immune to the global resurgence of antisemitism. It is incumbent upon all Australians—Jewish and non-Jewish alike—to reflect on their perceptions and challenge any biases they may unconsciously harbour. Recognising that anti-Zionism is a contemporary manifestation of antisemitism is a critical first step towards fostering a more inclusive and just society.

In conclusion, the "unconscious antisemite" may not recognise their prejudice, but ignorance does not absolve responsibility. Whether you are a bystander or an active participant in harmful rhetoric, silence and passivity are interpreted as consent. As Edmund Burke so aptly put it: "The only thing necessary for the triumph of evil is for good men to do nothing."

This is not just a fight for the Jewish community—it is a fight for the values that define us as Australians. Together, through education, advocacy, and collective resolve, we can confront and eradicate the insidious forms of antisemitism that threaten our society.

## Who is a Zionist?

In simple terms, a Zionist is someone who believes in the political and cultural self-determination of the indigenous people in their homeland. Am I a Zionist? You bet I am. But the better question to be asked is: Why isn't everyone?

6

# NEVER AGAIN MEANS NOW

## INTRODUCTION

Hatred thrives in silence. And too many people remain silent in the face of modern antisemitism.

For decades, Jewish communities have championed the causes of others—from Indigenous rights to refugee support. But when the Jewish community itself is under siege, where are the voices of those who once stood beside them? Where is the outrage? Where is the action?

This essay is a call to action, urging Australians—Jewish and non-Jewish alike—to take concrete steps to combat antisemitism, fight misinformation, and ensure that history does not repeat itself unchecked.

## WE HAVE AGENCY. LET'S USE IT!

*First published in The Australian Jewish News, December 12, 2024*

Hatred thrives in silence, and today, antisemitism is testing the resolve of Australia's moral compass. It's time to break the silence and take a stand for our Jewish community under siege.

Diaspora Jews have consistently demonstrated exceptional skill in advocating for others, but now is the time for Australians to step up and help a community under siege. In Australia, Jewish communities have championed causes such as Indigenous rights and equity under the law with notable success. Prominent Jewish Australians like Ron Castan AM QC, a leading barrister and human rights advocate, played a pivotal role in the landmark Mabo case, which recognised Indigenous land rights and fundamentally reshaped Australian legal and social frameworks. Similarly, Sir Isaac Isaacs, Australia's first Jewish Governor-General, was a steadfast advocate for national unity and justice, with a legacy that includes a commitment to Indigenous recognition and equity under the law. These significant contributions to broader societal causes highlight a commendable ethos of service. However, they stand in stark contrast to the community's apparent struggle to defend itself against the rising tide of antisemitism.

## What Is Antisemitism? It Is Criminal Abuse

Antisemitism is more than hatred—it is criminal abuse, and it must be treated as such. The International Holocaust Remembrance Alliance (IHRA) defines antisemitism as "a certain perception of Jews, which may be expressed as hatred toward Jews." This includes acts targeting Jewish individuals, institutions, or property, as well as Holocaust denial, demonisation of Israel, or holding Jews collectively responsible for Israel's actions.

Natan Sharansky's "3D Test" provides further clarity: Antisemitism is present in criticism of Israel that delegitimises its right to exist, demonises it with unfounded accusations, or applies double standards not used for other nations. This framework highlights the nuanced and insidious ways antisemitism infiltrates public discourse.

In Australia, antisemitism has escalated from rhetoric to violence. On December 5, 2024, as I wrote "The Baying Mob" for *The Australian Jewish News*, recounting fears inside The Great Synagogue in Sydney the previous night while protesters raged outside, another synagogue—Melbourne's Adass Israel—was soon thereafter attacked. These incidents reflect a dangerous trend of unchecked hatred trending towards terrorism.

## Advocacy From Early Allies

Advocacy for Israel and Jewish communities in Australia has found strong and diverse allies among influential non-Jewish Australians. Nova Peris, an Indigenous leader and former senator, has publicly denounced antisemitism, advocating for solidarity against hatred and drawing parallels between the histories of Jewish and Indigenous resilience. Warren Mundine, a prominent Indigenous Australian politician and commentator, has consistently supported Israel, recognising its democratic values and shared challenges in combating extremism.

Gemma Tognini, a columnist and media personality, has used her platform to call out antisemitism and highlight the need for Australians to stand with Jewish communities against rising prejudice. Chris Mitchell, a respected journalist and former editor-in-chief of *The Australian*, has been vocal in exposing media biases against Israel and advocating for balanced reporting on Middle Eastern conflicts. Mark Leach, an Anglican pastor, has fostered interfaith understanding by actively engaging with Jewish leaders and advocating for Israel's right to self-determination. Erin Molan, a prominent media personality and advocate, has lent her voice to combatting hatred and bigotry, including antisemitism, using her platform to champion inclusivity and call for accountability in public discourse.

These individuals exemplify a growing chorus of Australians standing up for justice, democracy, and the rights of Jewish communities. But their voices need your support as antisemitism is not just a Jewish issue—it is an Australian one.

## What to Do if You Witness Antisemitism

If you see antisemitic abuse, take the following steps:

- **Ensure Safety:** Help remove our Jewish friends from danger and call 000 for immediate threats.
- **Document and Report the Incident:** Record evidence, including photographs, screenshots, or written accounts. Note the time, location, and witnesses. Report the incident to police and anti-discrimination bodies.
- **Follow Up:** Keep records of correspondence and demand regular updates on your reporting. If dissatisfied, escalate concerns to your local MP or media outlets.

Beyond reporting incidents, participate in fostering interfaith dialogues, attending community events, and promoting educational initiatives about Jewish history and culture.

## It Is Time for Non-Jewish Australians to Take a Stand

Standing against antisemitism is not merely an act of solidarity—it is a defence of the core values that underpin Australian democracy: fairness, tolerance, and mutual respect. The alarming rise of antisemitism today bears an unsettling resemblance to the trends of the early twentieth century, where widespread indifference and inaction led to catastrophic consequences.

Whether by speaking out, offering support, or holding institutions and elected officials accountable for protecting all citizens, every Australian has a crucial role to play in ensuring that hatred finds no refuge in our nation. Together, we can uphold the principles of justice, equality, and unity that define the very best of Australia—because history has shown that when one community is targeted, the very fabric of society is at risk.

# CONCLUSION TO SECTION I

Antisemitism does not remain confined to Jews. History has shown that societies that tolerate it soon find themselves consumed by deeper moral decay, corruption, and collapse.

We are living through a pivotal moment. The world is making choices—to confront antisemitism or to tolerate it, to stand for truth or to surrender to lies, to defend civilisation or to let it crumble.

This section has exposed the resurgence of antisemitism in its many forms—violence, deception, ignorance, and complicity. But recognition is only the first step. Action is what matters.

The battles of today will shape the future. We must decide, now, which side of history we wish to be on.

# THE IRON SHIELD – ISRAEL'S DEFENCE AND ITS GLOBAL IMPLICATIONS

## INTRODUCTION TO SECTION II

For decades, Israel has stood as the lone democracy in a hostile region, a nation surrounded by adversaries who openly declare their intent to destroy it. Unlike any other country in the world, Israel must defend itself every single day—not only against conventional military threats but against terrorism, cyber warfare, and a relentless campaign of delegitimisation.

This section, The Iron Shield, explores Israel's security doctrine, military challenges, and the ethical dilemmas it faces. It examines not only how Israel defends itself, but how it is systematically vilified for doing what any other nation would consider a basic right—self-preservation.

The world demands of Israel what it demands of no other country: that it fight wars with zero casualties, against an enemy that hides behind civilians, all while under constant scrutiny from international organisations, hostile media, and ideological activists. And yet, despite these impossible expectations, Israel remains one of the most ethical military forces in history.

This section examines Israel's defence strategy, the morality of its military operations, and the global implications of its fight. For if Israel were ever to fall, it would not just be a tragedy for the Jewish people—it would be a harbinger of disaster for Western civilisation itself.

# 1

# SECURITY AT A COST: PROTECTOR OR PARADOX?

## INTRODUCTION

The Iron Dome is one of the most remarkable military innovations of our time. Designed to intercept and destroy incoming rockets, it has saved thousands of Israeli lives and prevented widespread devastation. But with its success comes an unintended consequence—the world now expects Israel to absorb endless attacks without responding decisively.

By neutralising Hamas and Hezbollah's rockets, the Iron Dome paradoxically shields Israel's enemies from the consequences of their aggression. It allows them to launch thousands of rockets with impunity, knowing that Israel's response will always be tempered by international pressure.

This essay examines the strategic paradox of the Iron Dome—how a defensive weapon designed to protect civilians has become, in some ways, a trap that restrains Israel's ability to end the conflict once and for all.

# SHIELD OR SNARE? THE STRATEGIC BURDEN OF ISRAEL'S "IRON DOME"

*First published in The Australian Jewish News, April 10, 2025*

One of contemporary Israel's most defining images is its extraordinary air defence system—a technological marvel developed out of necessity to counter relentless existential threats. This system stands as a testament to human ingenuity, resilience, and the high cost—both financial and emotional—of constant vigilance.

Yet, has this shield also become a snare? For decades, an ingenious and indigenous people—deeply rooted in their ancestral homeland and committed to peace—have been forced to tolerate the intolerable, trapped in a cycle of perpetual defence. The Iron Dome and its layered counterparts have provided a sense of security, but at what cost? Has Israel's technological mastery of missile defence inadvertently exacerbated the very threats it seeks to neutralise?

## The Double Standard: Israel's Unfair Burden

While no other nation would be expected to endure daily barrages of rockets, Israel is held to an impossible moral and strategic standard. Instead of global condemnation of Hamas's war crimes, Israel is pressured to show restraint, negotiate with terrorists, and accept periodic missile attacks as a fact of life.

This expectation was crystallised in April 2024, when US President Joe Biden adjured Israel to "take the win," referring to its successful missile defences against an Iranian drone and missile attack. The implication? That Israel should be content with swatting away incoming fire rather than eliminating the source of the threat. The expectation was not just unrealistic—it was ridiculous. No rational state would accept an endless barrage of enemy rockets as an acceptable status quo, yet Israel was effectively told to do just that. And not for the first time—Israel has been consistently and repeatedly expected to do just that.

This reductionist perspective—one that assumes Israel's defensive capabilities make aggression against it acceptable—ignores the human cost of resilience. Each intercepted rocket may prevent immediate loss of life, but it does not erase the trauma it leaves behind. A community is left shaken, living under the perpetual shadow of the next attack. A family is disrupted, forced to seek shelter at a moment's notice, their daily lives dictated by the whims of those who fire indiscriminately. A society is held hostage, conditioned to accept constant threat as an unavoidable reality rather than an aberration that demands decisive action.

This adds to the trauma of a population who endured the Second Intifada. The Second Intifada, also known as the Al-Aqsa Intifada, erupted in September 2000 and persisted until February 2005. This period was marked by intense violence, including numerous suicide bombings targeting buses, restaurants, and other public spaces within Israel. These attacks resulted in significant civilian casualties and widespread fear among the population. The relentless nature of these assaults profoundly traumatised Israeli society, leaving enduring psychological scars.

Beyond the immediate suffering, failing to confront aggression head-on emboldens adversaries to escalate their violence. History proves that unchallenged hostility does not fade—it festers. As General Douglas MacArthur once warned: "Appeasement begets new and bloodier wars."

Observers now have the benefit of hindsight: Ignoring threats does not neutralise them; it emboldens them. Each time Hamas, Hezbollah, or Iran launched an attack without decisive repercussions, they grew bolder, relentlessly probing Israel's red lines and testing global tolerance for their terror campaigns.

Yet, Western political elites and media figures consistently overlook these realities. Instead, they demand an unrealistic level of restraint from Israel while ignoring far more aggressive counterterrorism operations undertaken by other nations in the region.

## Purpose of This Article

This article provides an overview of Israel's extraordinary air defence system, examining both its strategic necessity and its unintended consequences. It exposes the opportunity cost of maintaining a technologically superior yet economically burdensome defence apparatus, questioning whether this reliance on interception alone has prolonged rather than resolved the threats Israel faces. Beyond the financial and psychological toll, the article explores how adversaries exploit this defensive posture to dictate the terms of engagement. Finally, it considers alternative approaches used in the region to defeat terrorism, contrasting Israel's measured responses with the decisive actions taken by its neighbours to neutralise similar threats.

## The Four Layers of Missile Defence

Israel's missile defence architecture operates on four interconnected layers:

- **Iron Dome** – The most well-known component, designed to intercept short-range rockets and artillery shells. It provides coverage for areas up to seventy kilometres, boasting a success rate often cited above 90 percent.

- **David's Sling** – A system for intercepting medium- to long-range missiles and drones, bridging the gap between the Iron Dome and higher-level defences.
- **Arrow 2 and Arrow 3** – Advanced interceptors designed to neutralise long-range ballistic missiles, including those carrying unconventional warheads.
- **Multi-Tier Coordination** – Systems that work in concert, guided by cutting-edge radar and tracking technologies to optimise resource deployment and ensure seamless coverage against a spectrum of threats.

While technologically extraordinary, these systems come at a staggering cost. The financial burden of maintaining, upgrading, and deploying these defences underscores Israel's unwavering commitment to safeguarding its population. However, it also highlights the asymmetric nature of Israel's conflicts.

## The Iron Dome's Economic Challenge

Each Iron Dome interceptor costs approximately US$50,000, whereas the rockets it intercepts—often crude and inexpensive—may cost as little as a few hundred dollars. This disparity underscores the economic challenge Israel faces in defending itself against asymmetric warfare.

During the May 2021 Gaza conflict, Hamas fired over 4,000 rockets at Israel. The Iron Dome intercepted 90 percent of those deemed a threat, reportedly costing Israel hundreds of millions of dollars. Beyond the financial toll, indirect costs—such as disruptions to daily life, economic activity, and psychological strain on civilians—further compound the burden.

Since October 2023, rocket fire from Gaza and Lebanon has surged, with estimates exceeding 7,000 rockets fired in the months following Hamas's coordinated attack. Each interception—while saving lives—adds to mounting defence expenditures.

An enemy only needs to "get lucky" once to penetrate air defences and strike a high-rise tower in Tel Aviv or critical infrastructure. Israel, however, must get lucky every time.

## Alternate Methods of Treatment

The challenge posed by Islamist terrorism is not unique to Israel. Other nations in the region have responded with overwhelming force and fewer restraints.

- **Jordan and Black September (1970):** In 1970, the Palestine Liberation Organization (PLO) operated within Jordan, posing a direct threat to the monarchy. In Black September, King Hussein launched a military crackdown, expelling PLO militants. The Jordanian army engaged in brutal urban warfare, decisively crushing PLO forces and forcing their relocation to Lebanon. An estimated 3,400 to 5,000 militants were killed.
- **Egypt, Saudi Arabia, and the UAE's Crackdown on Islamists:** Egypt under President Abdel Fattah el-Sisi has waged an aggressive crackdown on the Muslim Brotherhood, resulting in thousands of arrests and military operations that eliminated 1,000 to 2,000 militants.
- **Saudi Arabia and the UAE:** Both nations have aggressively targeted Islamist groups, restricting their activities and aligning their counterterrorism efforts with Egypt.

## Peace Through Strength

Such an approach found favour with Rabbi Meir Kahane, often referred to as the "militant rabbi." A controversial figure, Kahane was an outspoken advocate for Jewish self-defence and a staunch opponent of any concessions to terrorism. He famously declared: "If we ever hope to rid the world of the political AIDS of our time—terrorism—the rule must be clear: One does not deal with terrorists; one does not bargain with terrorists; one kills terrorists."

Kahane's views were polarising, and while some saw him as a visionary who spoke hard truths about security, others—both within and outside the Jewish community—condemned him as extremist, divisive, and dangerous. His Kach party was banned from Israeli politics for its radical positions, and he was ultimately assassinated in 1990 by El Sayyid Nosair, an Egyptian-born Islamist terrorist, in New York City. Nosair was later linked to the network that carried out the 1993 World Trade Center bombing, underscoring the very dangers of terrorism that Kahane had long warned about.

## Conclusion

Israel's multi-layered missile defence system, epitomised by the Iron Dome, is a testament to its ingenuity and resolve. However, this comes at a profound cost—financially, socially, and psychologically.

Reflecting on my military career, I have seen firsthand how complacency in defence can be lethal. Technology alone cannot eliminate threats. Warfare is a continuous cycle of adaptation—with adversaries constantly adjusting to bypass strengths and exploit weaknesses.

Perhaps one of America's founding fathers and first president, George Washington, said it best in 1799:

> *"Offensive operations, oftentimes, is the surest, if not the only…means of defence."*

# 2

# SURVIVORS SPEAK: FIRSTHAND ACCOUNTS OF GAZAN ATROCITIES

## INTRODUCTION

The October 7, 2023, massacre was not a military operation. It was a sadistic, genocidal attack on Israeli civilians. Hamas terrorists did not simply kill—they butchered, burnt, raped, and mutilated with a level of cruelty that defies comprehension.

What happened that day should have shocked the world into clarity. Instead, many in the West rushed to defend the perpetrators. University professors, journalists, and activists contorted themselves into grotesque justifications, blaming Israel for its own victimisation.

This essay provides firsthand accounts from the massacre and the subsequent war, cutting through the propaganda and exposing the reality of Israel's struggle for survival.

# FIRSTHAND ACCOUNTS OF GAZAN SAVAGERY AND BRUTALITY

*First published in The Australian Jewish News, March 27, 2025*

The events of October 7, 2023, will be remembered not only for their staggering brutality but also for the disturbing ideological forces that enabled such atrocities. The coordinated attack on Israel saw not only Hamas militants but also ordinary Gazans infiltrating Israeli communities, engaging in acts of violence that defy human comprehension.

Survivors' testimonies, intelligence reports, and even footage filmed by the perpetrators themselves paint a horrifying picture of a society radicalised to its core, where even so-called civilians took part in unspeakable savagery.

## The Reality of the October 7 Attacks

As the sun rose on October 7, under the cover of a massive rocket barrage, thousands of terrorists—by some reports 6,000—surged across the border into Israel by sea, air, and land.

The first wave consisted of heavily armed Hamas fighters, trained and equipped for urban warfare. Their detailed knowledge of Israeli homes, roads, and communities—which allowed them to navigate with precision—could only have been provided by Gazan workers who, until that moment, had been granted work visas as part of Israel's efforts to improve Gazan welfare and promote peaceful coexistence.

This malicious insider knowledge proved decisive. Terrorists targeted kibbutz armouries, vital infrastructure, and key defensive positions, ensuring that Israeli responders were quickly overwhelmed and communication lines to higher headquarters were severed. Many attackers disguised themselves in Israel

Defense Forces (IDF) uniforms, and some spoke Hebrew, further sowing confusion and chaos. Kibbutz security chiefs and quick response personnel—the first line of defence—were murdered in their homes or ambushed as they ran to retrieve weapons to protect their families.

Following this initial Hamas assault, Palestinian Islamic Jihad operatives—eager to claim their share of the bloodshed—joined the attack, further escalating the carnage.

But the two prescribed terrorist organisations were soon followed by another wave of attackers—masses of Gazan "civilians" armed with knives, hammers, and farm implements. These individuals looted, slaughtered, and desecrated with a level of cruelty that cannot be dismissed as mere opportunism.

This was not a spontaneous uprising—it was the culmination of decades of ideological indoctrination.

## "Civilians" as Perpetrators

Some of the most damning evidence comes not just from Hamas fighters, but from ordinary Gazans who actively participated in the massacre. This was not mere complicity—it was direct engagement in the slaughter, documented by the perpetrators themselves:

- Gazan civilians filmed their own crimes, proudly live-streaming and posting videos of their depravity.
- These were not isolated cases of looting or vandalism—they were deliberate massacres, carried out with sadistic pleasure.
- One video shows a Gazan man gleefully playing with the decapitated head of an Israeli farmer as his friends laugh and cheer.

- Another captures a father in Gaza parading the bloodied body of a kidnapped young woman in front of his cheering children, shouting that she was a gift from Allah.

- A group of civilians filmed themselves dragging a naked Israeli woman through the streets while chanting "Allahu Akbar," kicking her motionless body and spitting on her.

- A terrorist used an Israeli victim's phone to call his parents and proudly boast about murdering ten Jews. In the recorded call, he exclaims, "I killed ten with my own hands! Your son killed Jews!" His parents respond with congratulations and blessings.

- At least one terrorist uploaded the murder of a woman to her Facebook page, which is how her family discovered what had happened to her.

- A terrorist filmed a video of them decapitating a Thai worker with a spade.

This depravity was not limited to Hamas fighters. Ordinary Gazans—men and women alike—actively took part in the bloodshed. Some brought their children to witness and celebrate the slaughter, ensuring that another generation would be poisoned by hatred and brutality.

## Testimonies of the Survivors

One survivor, a young woman taken hostage from the Nova music festival, later recounted the taunts and abuse she endured—not only from Hamas fighters but from children as young as ten.

*"They spat at me, cursed at me, called me a Jew-pig. They had no hesitation, no fear, just hatred."*

Another survivor, an elderly man from Kfar Aza, described how his neighbours were burnt alive while Gazans filmed the carnage, cheering.

*"This was not the behaviour of desperate people seeking freedom; it was the product of a society conditioned to dehumanise Jews."*

## Rape as a Weapon of War

Captured Hamas operatives have confessed to the widespread, systematic use of rape as a weapon of terror during the attack.

One interrogated terrorist detailed how women were gang-raped and mutilated before being executed.

*"The orders were clear—break them, humiliate them, make them suffer,"* he admitted.

Multiple witnesses, including forensic experts, have described how Israeli women's bodies were found with their pelvises shattered—clear evidence of extreme sexual violence.

Some victims were filmed being brutalised by their attackers before being set on fire or shot.

## The Role of Ideological Indoctrination

For years, many in the West have clung to the comforting notion that a clear distinction exists between Gaza's militants and its civilians.

Yet, the testimonies of hostages and survivors challenge this assumption. The hatred ingrained in Gazan society is not accidental—it is cultivated through a state-sponsored system of propaganda. Schools teach martyrdom as a noble pursuit, summer camps train children for jihad, and media outlets glorify the murder of Jews, ensuring that each new generation is indoctrinated with hatred from an early age.

Mia Schem, a French Israeli woman who spent fifty-four days as a Hamas hostage, later revealed the chilling indoctrination she observed firsthand.

> *"Even the children—they knew how to hate. It's all they've ever been taught."*

Another released hostage reported that her captors, far from expressing remorse, viewed their crimes as acts of divine justice.

More recently, Gazan women have openly boasted about their involvement in holding Israeli hostages. One woman proudly declared that she kept kidnapped Israelis in her home, feeding them scraps while her husband and sons joined the massacre. Another, when asked if she regretted her involvement, laughed and said, "We would do it again."

Maya Angelou famously said, "When people show you who they are, believe them."

## The Violation of International Humanitarian Law

The scale and nature of the atrocities committed on October 7 constitute clear violations of international humanitarian law.

The Geneva Conventions prohibit

- targeting civilians,
- sexual violence as a weapon of war,
- the taking of hostages, and
- the desecration of the dead.

Hamas and the civilians who participated in the massacres committed war crimes of the most egregious nature.

Yet, much of the international community has responded with moral equivocation.

Instead of unequivocally condemning Hamas, many Western politicians and academics have sought to shift blame onto Israel, arguing that these crimes were an inevitable consequence of the "occupation"—a blatant falsehood, given that Israel unilaterally withdrew from Gaza in 2005.

To put it plainly: There is no justification under international law for what happened on October 7. Rape, murder, mutilation, and hostage-taking are not acts of "resistance"—they are war crimes.

And those who excuse or minimise these horrors are complicit in their perpetuation.

## The Danger of Western Denial

Despite overwhelming evidence, many in the West continue to downplay the scale of Gaza's radicalisation.

This refusal to confront reality is not just misguided—it is dangerous.

If Western nations fail to acknowledge the extent of radicalisation in Gaza, they risk importing the very ideologies that led to October 7.

The mass celebrations of Hamas's attack in cities like London, Sydney, and New York should serve as a dire warning that this problem is not confined to the Middle East.

## The Path Forward

To solve a problem, one must first understand its true nature.

The world must recognise that the October 7 atrocities were not driven by political grievances but by a deeply ingrained hatred that has been nurtured for generations—with Western aid funding much of this infrastructure and indoctrination.

The voices of the survivors tell a story—one that demands to be heard, no matter how uncomfortable it may be.

# 3

# THE WAR ON INNOCENCE: A NAME THAT MUST NOT BE FORGOTTEN

## INTRODUCTION

Behind every statistic is a human life.

The tragedy of the Israeli struggle is not just in its battles but in the stories of the individuals who are caught in them. Yarden Bibas was not just a name. He was a husband, a father, a son. He was part of a family whose suffering is mirrored in the grief of countless others.

This essay provides a deeply personal perspective on the victims of Hamas terrorism, focusing on the human cost of war that often gets lost in the political debates and military analyses.

By telling Yarden's story, we reaffirm why Israel fights—not for power, not for revenge, but for the right of its people to live free from fear and destruction.

## IN THIS, I AM YARDEN BIBAS

*First published in The Australian Jewish News, February 21, 2025*

The tragic fate of the Bibas family stands as a harrowing testament to the barbarism unleashed upon Israel on October 7, 2023. Yarden Bibas, 34, his wife Shiri, 32, and their two young children—Ariel, 4, and Kfir, just 9 months old—were abducted from their home in Kibbutz Nir Oz by Gazan civilians—not Hamas or Palestinian Islamic Jihad—and violently dragged into the depths of Gaza's depravity. Their unimaginable suffering, and the brutal way the bodies of a loving mother and her two innocent boys were returned to Israel 502 days later, exposes not only the degeneracy of Hamas but also the moral collapse of those who refuse to acknowledge it.

The images of the Bibas family have been burnt into the global conscience. Red-haired baby Kfir, cradled in the arms of his terrified mother, became a heartbreaking symbol of innocence shattered by cruelty. Their abduction was not just an attack on one family—it was an assault on humanity itself. And yet, in parts of the world, there was no universal outrage. Instead, there were celebrations in the streets of Gaza, university protests in the West portraying Hamas as the victim, and a deafening silence from international institutions that claim to uphold human rights.

The fate of the Bibas family is not just a tragedy—it is a moral litmus test for the world. If the cold-blooded murder of an infant, a four-year-old child, and their mother fails to provoke universal condemnation, then what does?

## The Depravity of Hamas's Actions

The story of the Bibas family did not end with their abduction. For months, their fate remained uncertain, their names whispered in desperate prayers. Then, on February 20, 2025, Hamas staged a grotesque spectacle, parading their coffins through Khan Younis before handing them over to the Red Cross. The coffins were locked, bearing the names and images of Shiri and her children, a final insult to their dignity.

This act was not an outlier—it was the culmination of decades of radicalisation in Gaza. The international community, through institutions like the United Nations Relief and Works Agency (UNRWA), has funded an education system that indoctrinates children with violent Jew-hatred from infancy. In such a society, there is no moral reckoning when a baby is murdered—only a twisted sense of victory.

## A Personal Reckoning

For those of us who have spent time in Israel, who have walked its streets and lived among its people, the fate of the Bibas family feels deeply personal. I find it impossible to witness such horror and remain a bystander.

I have served my country—Australia—for thirty years as a soldier in the Australian Army, dedicating my life to understanding and countering threats. In doing so, I have encountered evil before, but rarely has it been so openly embraced by those who should be held accountable. The lack of outrage from Western leaders, the equivocation from international bodies, and the media's willingness to entertain Hamas's propaganda all reveal a dangerous reality: We are losing our moral compass.

## The Path Forward

The murder of the Bibas family should be a watershed moment, forcing the world to confront the true nature of Hamas and the radicalised culture it has fostered in Gaza. But outrage is not enough.

The West must cease its funding of institutions that perpetuate extremism. Governments must take a hard stance against those who glorify terrorism within their own borders. And most importantly, we must never allow ourselves to become desensitised to this horror. The moment we rationalise such evil, we open the door for it to spread.

The Bibas family was targeted because they were Israeli and because they were Jewish. Their deaths were celebrated because their killers had been raised to believe that such atrocities are justified. If we fail to acknowledge the ideological war being waged against civilisation itself, we will soon find ourselves the next targets.

I grieve for Yarden Bibas, for Shiri, for Ariel, and for baby Kfir. And in this, I am Yarden Bibas.

# 4

# COLLATERAL BY DESIGN: HOW HAMAS WEAPONISES CIVILIANS

## INTRODUCTION

No terrorist organisation in modern history has perfected the use of human shields quite like Hamas. It is not merely a byproduct of urban warfare—it is a deliberate strategy. Hamas embeds its weapons in hospitals, schools, and mosques, knowing that Israel, bound by its ethical code, will hesitate before striking.

Western media plays into this strategy, portraying every Hamas operative as an innocent civilian and treating terrorist strongholds as humanitarian sites. The result? Israel is damned no matter what it does—criticised for responding yet expected to tolerate constant attacks on its people.

This essay exposes the moral depravity of Hamas, the complicity of international organisations, and the absurd double standards imposed on Israel.

# TARGETED HUMAN SACRIFICE

*First published in The Australian Jewish News, February 23, 2025*

The unilateral withdrawal of the Israel Defense Forces (IDF) from Gaza in 2005 marked a pivotal moment in the region's history. Intended to pave the way for Palestinian self-determination, the withdrawal instead enabled Hamas to transform Gaza into a launchpad for terror. Hamas's grotesque strategy of cynically sacrificing its own population, termed "targeted human sacrifice," demands international scrutiny and condemnation.

## A Legacy of Violence

Since 2005, Hamas and Palestinian Islamic Jihad have launched tens of thousands of rockets at Israeli civilians, a blatant violation of international law prohibiting attacks on non-combatants. Richard Kemp, a former commander of British forces in Afghanistan, aptly describes this as a "dual war crime strategy": attacking civilians while using their own people as human shields.

For Israelis, prior to October 7, 2023, this meant living under constant threat, with air raid sirens and bomb shelters embedded into daily life. In stark contrast, Hamas constructed no shelters for Gazans, instead investing in terror tunnels and weapon stockpiles hidden beneath schools, hospitals, and mosques. This deliberate exposure of civilians to danger highlights Hamas's disregard for human life.

## Exploiting Protected Infrastructure

Civilian infrastructure, such as hospitals, schools, and places of worship, are afforded protected status under the laws of armed conflict. However, as Natasha Hausdorff, a barrister specialising in international law, notes: "When such facilities are used for military purposes, these protections are nullified." Hamas flagrantly exploits this, embedding military assets in civilian areas, making hospitals and schools legitimate military targets under international law.

During Operation Protective Edge in 2014, the IDF discovered rockets hidden in United Nations-run schools. This pattern has intensified, with hospitals being used as command centres and residential buildings storing weapons. These actions endanger Palestinian civilians, present Israel with excruciating moral dilemmas, and cost IDF soldiers their lives.

## The Strategy of Human Shields

Hamas's use of human shields is not a defensive necessity but a calculated strategy to weaponise international sympathy. Douglas Murray, a noted commentator, explains: "By placing civilians in harm's way, Hamas creates the illusion of disproportionate harm to generate outrage against Israel."

John Spencer, Chair of Urban Warfare Studies at the Modern War Institute, highlights the challenges this tactic imposes: "When combatants use densely populated urban areas to shield their operations, they exploit the ethical frameworks of their adversaries." This cynical strategy feeds Hamas's propaganda machine, relying on harrowing imagery of civilian casualties to stoke anti-Israel sentiment.

It is a tragic indictment of Western naivety that so many have swallowed—hook, line, and sinker—this manipulative narrative.

## The Absence of Shelters in Gaza

Unlike Israel, which has ensured widespread access to bomb shelters, Hamas has built none for Gaza's civilians. Andrew Fox, a former British Army officer, underscores this disparity: "It's not a matter of resources but priorities. Hamas prioritises weapons over the welfare of its people."

This deliberate neglect leaves Gazans defenceless during Israeli counter strikes, compounding their suffering. Hamas then exploits these tragedies for propaganda, obscuring its own culpability.

In September 2024, I was personally briefed on the IDF's extraordinary efforts to minimise civilian casualties. In Rafah, southern Gaza, the IDF successfully eliminated over 1,000 terrorists while civilian casualties were limited to twenty-four.

Such precision in dense urban warfare is unprecedented and a testament to the IDF's ethical commitment—an inconvenient truth for antisemites and ideologically motivated critics in mainstream media and academia.

## How Does the IDF Minimise Civilian Casualties?

The IDF employs many strategies to minimise civilian casualties in Gaza. These include issuing advance warnings through leaflets, phone calls, and text messages to alert residents of impending operations, allowing them time to evacuate. The IDF also uses precision-guided munitions to accurately target militant positions while avoiding civilian areas. Additionally, tactics like "roof-knocking"—firing non-lethal munitions onto roofs as a warning before a strike—are utilised to prompt evacuations. The IDF further establishes humanitarian corridors to facilitate safe civilian movement away from conflict zones. These measures reflect the IDF's commitment to reducing harm to non-combatants during military operations.

## The Calculus of Death

For Hamas, civilian casualties are not collateral damage but a deliberate tactic. Richard Kemp observes: "Hamas' greatest weapon is not its rockets or tunnels but its ability to manipulate world opinion. Civilian casualties are central to their strategy."

This chilling calculus involves positioning military assets in residential areas and coercing civilians to remain in harm's way, ensuring a high death toll during Israeli strikes.

## Legal and Moral Clarity

Under international law, the responsibility for civilian casualties lies with the party that uses civilians as shields. Hamas's tactics constitute war crimes, as Andrew Fox asserts: "The international community must hold Hamas accountable for its actions."

Yet global responses often fail to reflect this reality, with media narratives disproportionately criticising Israel while ignoring Hamas's culpability. This imbalance perpetuates misinformation and emboldens Hamas to continue its cynical strategies.

## A Call to Action

Those advocating for a ceasefire in the current conflict must reflect deeply on the implications of their stance. A more constructive approach would be to demand the arrest and prosecution of Hamas leaders worldwide by the International Criminal Court (ICC), which holds jurisdiction to try individuals for war crimes and crimes against humanity.

Accountability and simplicity should guide international action. If the ICC fails to take immediate and decisive measures against Hamas leaders globally, it should be defunded and its ineffectual leadership replaced. Furthermore, Hamas assets, wherever they exist, must be seized and redirected to Israel to help offset the cost of humanitarian aid for those affected in the Gaza Envelope. Nations such as Qatar and Türkiye, which harbour or have harboured Hamas leaders, must face stringent international sanctions and be compelled to pay reparations to Israel.

The global community must confront Hamas's egregious strategy of targeted human sacrifice for what it truly is: a heinous and calculated effort to maximise civilian suffering for political gain. This starts with holding Hamas accountable under international law and rejecting the false equivalence between a democracy defending its citizens and a terrorist organisation exploiting its own people.

The consequences for nation-states, media outlets, individuals, or transnational organisations that support Hamas must be swift and severe. Tolerating such actions perpetuates the cycle of violence and suffering. Equally, the people of Gaza deserve better than the banal voices in the West, manipulated by Hamas propaganda into endorsing an ill-considered strategy that ultimately harms everyone involved.

Douglas Murray astutely observes:

"The tragedy of Gaza is not that it is blockaded
by Israel but that it is held hostage by Hamas."

The people of Gaza deserve better—not as pawns in a propaganda war but as human beings entitled to peace, dignity, and a future free from tyranny.

Addressing this crisis demands courage, clarity, and an unwavering commitment to the truth.

# 5

# STRENGTHENING ISRAEL'S VOICE

## INTRODUCTION

Israel excels at self-defence but struggles in the information war. Despite its military successes, it has failed to communicate its story effectively to the world. Its adversaries, meanwhile, master the art of propaganda, emotional manipulation, and misinformation.

The world sees Israel as a powerful military state while ignoring the existential threats it faces. The reality is that Israel is fighting for its very survival, yet too many in the West remain indifferent—or worse, sympathetic to its enemies.

This essay argues that Israel does not just need weapons and diplomacy—it needs advocates. It needs people who understand the truth and are willing to fight for it in the media, in academia, and in the corridors of power.

## "GOOD MUSIC, INADEQUATE SPEAKERS" – ISRAEL NEEDS OUR HELP

*First published in The Australian Jewish News, November 7, 2024*

This article was written in Jerusalem after a profoundly insightful visit to Israel with the European Leadership Network (ELNET). ELNET is a non-profit organisation dedicated to strengthening relations between Europe and Israel by promoting cooperation on political, security, and strategic issues. From September 1 to 6, 2024, ELNET hosted a Military Expert Panel composed of veterans and prominent figures from Australia, Canada, France, Romania, the United Kingdom, and the United States.

The Panel received briefings from the Israeli Government, the Israel Defense Forces (IDF), various think tanks, and non-governmental organisations, with access at the highest levels. Meetings included discussions with Prime Minister Netanyahu, Defense Minister Gallant, Knesset Member Yuli Edelstein, and Major General Goldfus, former commander of the 92nd Division operating in Gaza.

The Panel visited Kibbutz Kfar Aza, the Nahal Oz military base, and Re'im, the site of the Supernova Music Festival, all devastated by terrorists on October 7. The Panel also toured Gaza along the Philadelphi Corridor, witnessing firsthand some of the 200 tunnels discovered so far between Gaza and Egypt.

Three key points struck me during my time in Israel. First, there is currently no viable peace process between Israelis and Palestinians, although the Abraham Accords and rapprochement with Saudi Arabia remain on track. Second, Hamas has transformed Gaza into a highly fortified stronghold, far beyond what I could have imagined. Finally, the morale and resilience of the IDF and the broader Israeli population are both moving and inspiring, especially as they face existential military threats from Iran and disinformation campaigns from biased media and antisemites.

Upon returning to Australia, I see Israel as a nation creating "great music" that is, unfortunately, being broadcast through "inadequate speakers." I encourage readers to visit Israel, witness the truth firsthand, and, upon returning, help amplify Israel's message by correcting misinformation with facts. In my judgement, at this challenging time, while Israel requires the support of the world, it is the world that perhaps needs Israel even more. The terror and ideology that Israel is fighting threaten us all, making Israel's battle one of global significance.

## The Failed Peace Process and the Abraham Accords

Dr. Einat Wilf, a prominent Israeli intellectual and former politician, has authored several books, including *The War of Return: How Western Indulgence of the Palestinian Dream Has Obstructed the Path to Peace*. In a post on September 8, 2024, Wilf quotes an unnamed US negotiator who said, "After thirty years, there was never a negotiation." According to him, Israel made offers, but Arafat—and later Abbas—repeatedly said no. Negotiations were mostly between the US and Israel, with the US pressing Israel to offer more without determining whether the Palestinians were willing to accept the Jewish state.

The two-state solution now feels unsafe to many who once supported it. After spending an evening with Itamar Marcus, director of Palestinian Media Watch, it became clear why. In his compelling presentation, Marcus explained that antisemitism is ingrained in the Palestinian national identity, and the official policy remains the destruction of Israel. This reality is inconvenient for those pushing for Palestinian recognition without mutual obligation.

It is alarming that Western media often ignore Palestinian Authority (PA) policies like payments to the families of terrorists. Additionally, Mahmoud Abbas has not condemned the October 7 massacre carried out by Hamas, instead blaming Israel. Prime Minister Netanyahu has criticised Abbas for his failure to condemn the attack and for spreading disinformation about Israel's responsibility.

The Abraham Accords facilitated historic normalisation agreements between Israel and several Arab states. There is a level of confidence within Israel that countries including Saudi Arabia and Indonesia are close to normalizing relations in the next decade.

The US Obama administration initially believed that peace between Israel and the Palestinians should come before normalisation with the broader Arab world. This position was based on the belief that resolving the Israeli-Palestinian conflict was central to regional peace. Obama's administration emphasised the two-state solution and pressured Israel to halt settlement activity in the West Bank as a way to revive direct negotiations with the Palestinians.

However, this approach shifted with the signing of the Abraham Accords under the Trump administration, which showed that normalisation with Arab states could proceed independently of progress on the Palestinian issue. Obama's earlier emphasis on a Palestinian-Israeli settlement as a prerequisite for wider Arab-Israeli peace was overtaken by changing dynamics, including shared concerns between Israel and Gulf states over Iran's regional activities and economic cooperation potential.

These countries view Iran as a destabilizing force, and cooperation between Riyadh and Jerusalem could bolster their collective security efforts. Economically, normalisation with Israel offers Saudi Arabia access to Israeli technology, particularly in sectors like defence, cybersecurity, agriculture, and renewable energy, aligning with Saudi Vision 2030's goal to diversify its economy.

Additionally, formal ties could open avenues for US support and investment, strengthening Saudi Arabia's global position. However, the kingdom remains cautious, balancing its regional leadership role and domestic considerations, particularly its longstanding support for the Palestinian cause. Despite these complexities, the geopolitical advantages, including countering Iranian aggression and accessing significant economic benefits, make Saudi participation in the Abraham Accords a real possibility as regional dynamics evolve.

## Hamas's Transformation of Gaza

The IDF fully withdrew from Gaza on September 12, 2005, as part of Israel's disengagement plan. Hamas took control in 2007 after a brief power-sharing government with Fatah, and since then has fortified Gaza extensively. Over 480 kilometres of Hamas tunnels have been discovered, and the battlefield in Gaza is one of the most complex in modern warfare.

The IDF's learning curve has been steep, evolving from avoiding tunnel engagement to dominating the underground labyrinth. IDF operations now involve clearing over 1,000 meters of tunnels per night. Many tunnels, designed for evasion rather than combat, feature infrastructure like kitchens and even cages for hostages. Hamas has clustered its military assets in civilian areas, including mosques, hospitals, and schools, forcing the IDF to take extraordinary measures to avoid civilian casualties.

In Rafah alone, 13.6 kilometres of tunnels have been destroyed, along with hundreds of shafts and infrastructure nodes. The damage to urban infrastructure is significant, but civilian casualties have been minimal thanks to the IDF's efforts to relocate non-combatants before major operations. This contrasts starkly with battles like the Second Battle of Fallujah in Iraq (2004), where the ratio of civilian deaths to combatant deaths was much higher.

The behaviour, restraint, and ethics of IDF soldiers are unparalleled in the history of warfare. One anecdote tells of an IDF sniper who had precisely neutralised over one hundred terrorists in Gaza, yet received a commendation not for his combat prowess, but for an extraordinary act of humanity. When a Hamas terrorist forced a civilian youth into the sniper's line of fire, hoping for the death of the innocent, the sniper managed to manoeuvre, separate, and save the youth from harm.

Several IDF soldiers shared that they fight not with hatred, but with love in their hearts—love for their country, Israel, and for their fellow Israelis. This ethos is not confined to Jewish Israelis; some of the finest, fiercest, and bravest IDF soldiers come from the Druze community. In my thirty years in the profession of arms, I have infrequently encountered soldiers of this calibre. The level of education exhibited by both regular and reserve IDF personnel is beyond comparison.

The IDF stands as a technologically advanced, professional, motivated, and ethical fighting force, which compares favourably against the findings of Justice Paul Brereton's recent investigation into alleged misconduct by another military force.

## The Resilience of Israel

As a gentile, I was unaccustomed to Jewish holidays, but I smiled when friends explained that many holidays commemorate survival: "They tried to kill us. We survived. Let's eat!" This resilience was clear again following the horrors of October 7, which left deep scars across Israel.

As of early September 2024, about 101 hostages remain in Gaza, ninety-seven of whom were abducted on October 7. Hamas has used hostage negotiations to increase pressure on Israeli leadership, leading to deep divides within the country.

On September 1, 2024, the Histadrut labour federation led a mass protest over the government's failure to secure the hostages' release. Hundreds of thousands of Israelis participated in a general strike, showing solidarity with the hostages' families. Now is not the time for division within Israel; unity is critical in the face of such profound challenges.

The actions of Hamas amount to psychological and physical torture. Their demands for a ceasefire and the release of Palestinian prisoners in exchange for hostages are impossible for Israel to accept. Rewarding such behaviour only perpetuates a cycle of terror.

During my recent visit to Israel, I witnessed resilience in the face of unimaginable challenges. I encourage all those who support Israel to visit, to educate, and to advocate. Israel has a remarkable story to tell, and it is our duty to ensure that story is heard. Am Yisrael Chai.

6

# STANDING TALL: RESISTING THE PRESSURES OF ANTISEMITISM

## INTRODUCTION

Israel operates under conditions no other country in history has faced. It fights wars against an enemy that does not abide by any laws of war, yet is held to higher ethical standards than any military force in history. It is condemned for defending itself, yet expected to accept terrorism as a fact of life.

The expectations placed on Israel are absurd: Win wars without harming civilians, tolerate existential threats indefinitely, and seek peace with those who seek its destruction. The reality is that Israel is often forced to make impossible choices, balancing military necessity with moral responsibility.

This essay explores the complex ethical dilemmas Israel faces, from targeted killings to counterinsurgency operations, and asks whether any other country would act with the same restraint.

# IMPOSSIBLE PRESSURES: LET'S DO BETTER, AUSTRALIA!

*First published in The Australian Jewish News, January 2, 2025*

## Introduction

There exists an uncomfortable reality in Australia: antisemitic views held by individuals of Jewish heritage. For many, the notion seems paradoxical—how could members of a community shaped by millennia of persecution and the trauma of the Holocaust internalise antisemitism? Yet, this phenomenon is real and demands exploration.

While entrenched views among some individuals may be difficult to change, young Jewish Australians face unique and urgent challenges. Navigating immense pressures compounded by biased narratives in media and society, they require understanding and support. Non-Jewish Australians must recognise these challenges and take responsibility for alleviating them.

This article calls for reflection and action, anchored in the universal ethic: "Do unto others as you would have them do unto you."

## The Historical Roots of Jewish Antisemitism

The term "self-hating Jew" has long been used to describe individuals who reject or disparage their Jewish identity. Theodor Lessing's *Der jüdische Selbsthaß* (1930) explored how societal rejection forces some Jews to internalise antisemitic attitudes. Psychologist Kurt Lewin observed that such individuals often long for acceptance by the majority, leading them to reject their heritage.

Today, this manifests as alignment with anti-Zionist ideologies, where Jewish individuals join movements that delegitimise Israel or apply double standards to its policies. By doing so, they unintentionally contribute to an ecosystem of antisemitic rhetoric.

## The Burden on Young Jewish Australians

Young Jewish Australians are caught in a moral dilemma, exacerbated by mainstream media and social platforms that amplify antisemitic narratives under the guise of legitimate critique. Trusted outlets like the Australian Broadcasting Corporation (ABC), once seen as credible, have contributed to an environment where young Jews feel forced to choose between their cultural identity and social acceptance.

This untenable position worsened after the Hamas terror attacks of October 7, 2023. Non-Jewish Australians who perpetuate this dynamic bear responsibility for creating a quagmire that alienates and isolates young Jewish Australians.

## What Is Zionism?

At its core, Zionism advocates for the political and cultural self-determination of the Jewish people in their ancestral homeland. Historically, this was not a universal aspect of Jewish identity, and some Jewish groups continue to critique Zionism based on ideological, ethical, or theological grounds.

**Religious Anti-Zionism:** Groups like Neturei Karta oppose Zionism for theological reasons, believing that a Jewish state should not exist until the arrival of the Messiah. While their opposition stems from religious convictions, it fails to address modern realities of Jewish vulnerability.

**Ethical Critiques:** Groups like Jewish Voice for Peace oppose Zionism as conflicting with values of justice and equality. However, their singular focus on Israel ignores accountability for Palestinian leadership and human rights abuses, reflecting a bias that undermines Jewish self-determination.

**Historical Perspectives:** Movements like the Jewish Bund prioritised cultural and political autonomy in the diaspora over nationalism. While rooted in a rich tradition of debate, such perspectives do not account for the lessons of history: Without sovereignty, Jewish safety cannot be guaranteed.

## The Line Between Critique and Antisemitism

Criticising Israeli policies is legitimate; denying Israel's right to exist is antisemitic. When Jewish anti-Zionists align with movements seeking to dismantle Israel, they empower actors who are not concerned with justice but with eroding Jewish sovereignty.

## International Bias Against Israel

Sustained international scrutiny of Israel often crosses the line into antisemitism:

- **UN Resolutions:** The United Nations Human Rights Council (UNHRC) passes more resolutions against Israel than against nations with systemic abuses, such as North Korea or Syria.
- **Selective Standards:** Territorial disputes like Tibet or Kashmir receive far less attention than Israeli settlements.

This disproportionate focus creates a cultural narrative where young Jews feel pressured to disavow Zionism to gain social acceptance. It fosters a false choice: Abandon support for Jewish sovereignty or face social exclusion.

## A Strange Coalition

Modern antisemitism emerges from an unlikely coalition of Islamists, Marxists, anarchists, and hard-left zealots. Despite their ideological differences, these groups unite in disdain for Israel. Within this alliance, some individuals exploit their Jewish heritage to attack their own community.

As Douglas Murray stated, "Those who say the Jewish state alone is illegitimate are not simply anti-Zionist but antisemitic." Natasha Hausdorff adds, "Anti-Zionism is antisemitism because it singles out Jewish self-determination for opprobrium."

Paradoxically, communities familiar with oppression—such as Iranians, Copts, and Kurds—often support Zionism, recognising its role in self-determination. Meanwhile, some Australians influenced by ideological trends perpetuate antisemitism, passively or actively.

## What Can Non-Jewish Australians Do?

To combat rising antisemitism, Australia must prioritise accountability, education, and solidarity:

- **Accountability:** Antisemitism in politics, universities, and media must be addressed. Politicians and officials who fail to act against attacks on Jewish institutions should resign or be removed.
- **Education:** Campaigns highlighting the contributions and resilience of Jewish Australians can combat ignorance and foster understanding.

- **Solidarity:** Non-Jewish Australians must stand against hate. As Edmund Burke warned, "The only thing necessary for the triumph of evil is for good men to do nothing." Allyship strengthens society and counters prejudice.

## A Call to Action

The Jewish people's history is one of resilience and meaningful debate. As the Late Rabbi Lord Jonathan Sacks said, "If we want to fight antisemitism, let us walk tall and proud as Jews, and let us work with all humanity to banish hatred forever."

To Jewish Australians, stand tall and embrace your identity. To non-Jewish Australians, stand with the Jewish community and help young Jewish Australians move beyond the "Sophie's Choice" they often face—a heartbreaking dilemma between cultural identity and social acceptance. No one should have to choose between being true to themselves and being embraced by society.

As the Talmud teaches, "If I am not for myself, who will be for me? If not now, when?" Let us act now to create a society where young Australians, regardless of their background, can thrive without fear or compromise.

# CONCLUSION TO SECTION II

Israel's military struggle is not just about defending its borders—it is about defending the very concept of civilisation itself. The enemies Israel faces do not merely want land; they want to destroy a free society built on democracy, human rights, and religious tolerance.

Yet, Israel is expected to fight this battle alone, constrained by double standards, diplomatic pressures, and ideological hostility. The hypocrisy of the world is staggering; nations that have waged brutal wars now lecture Israel on morality, while terrorist organisations are given the benefit of the doubt.

But Israel will endure. It will continue to fight, not just for itself, but for the values that underpin Western civilisation.

Who will stand with Israel in this fight?

# THE WAR OF PERCEPTION – MISINFORMATION, MEDIA BIAS, AND THE NARRATIVE BATTLE

## INTRODUCTION TO SECTION III

Wars are not just fought on battlefields; they are fought in the minds of people. Israel's most dangerous war is not military—it is the war of perception.

Israel faces an unprecedented campaign of misinformation, manipulation, and outright deceit. Its enemies understand that they cannot defeat the Israel Defense Forces (IDF) through conventional warfare, so they attack Israel through propaganda, media bias, and historical revisionism. The goal is simple:

Delegitimise Israel, turn world opinion against it, and weaken its ability to defend itself.

This section explores the tactics used to distort reality; the role of academia, social media, and mainstream news outlets in spreading lies; and the dangers of moral relativism in shaping public opinion.

At its core, this war is not just about Israel. It is about truth itself. If we allow fact to be replaced by fiction, if we permit terrorists to be painted as freedom fighters and democracies to be vilified as aggressors, then civilisation itself is at risk.

1

# HOW PROPAGANDA FUELS ANTI-ISRAEL LIES

## INTRODUCTION

The techniques of gaslighting and projection, famously described in George Orwell's *1984*, are central to the anti-Israel propaganda machine.

Gaslighting distorts reality to make people doubt what they see with their own eyes.

Projection shifts blame from the guilty to the innocent, allowing aggressors to masquerade as victims.

Israel is gaslit into believing it is the problem, even as it fights to protect its civilians. Hamas projects its own war crimes onto Israel, accusing the Jewish state of genocide even as it deliberately targets and murders innocent Jews.

This essay exposes how these Orwellian tactics are weaponised against Israel, how journalists and academics fuel the deception, and why it is imperative to reclaim the truth.

# GASLIGHTING AND PROJECTION OF ORWELLIAN PROPORTION

*First published in The Australian Jewish News, December 20, 2024*

The Israel Defense Forces (IDF) finds itself engaged in a pivotal and agonising conflict in Gaza following the unspeakable atrocities perpetrated by Hamas on October 7, 2023. This war, however, extends far beyond the battlefield; it is also an information war of staggering proportions. At the heart of this struggle lie two psychological tactics—gaslighting and projection—employed on a scale that brings to mind George Orwell's dystopian warnings in *1984*. This article explores these concepts, Hamas's manipulation of casualty narratives, the infiltration of institutions like the United Nations Relief and Works Agency (UNRWA), and the failures of journalistic integrity that exacerbate these falsehoods.

## Gaslighting, Projection, and Orwell's Legacy

Gaslighting is a manipulative tactic where reality is distorted, causing individuals to doubt their own understanding of events. Originating from Patrick Hamilton's play *Gas Light*, the term now refers to psychological manipulation at scale. Similarly, projection involves attributing one's own unacceptable behaviours to others, a tactic of deflection that shifts blame while masking the truth.

Orwell's *1984* provides a chilling framework for understanding these tactics in modern conflict: Propaganda, rewriting history, and suppressing dissent have become key tools in the war of perception. Today, Hamas exploits these methods to manipulate narratives, spread disinformation, and obscure its culpability.

## Hamas's False Narratives and Casualty Manipulation

Hamas-controlled sources, such as the Gaza Ministry of Health (MoH), systematically inflate casualty figures by failing to distinguish between civilians and combatants, over-reporting fatalities among women and children, and even including deaths unrelated to the conflict. Major Andrew Fox's report *Questionable Counting*, published by the Henry Jackson Society, reveals how these distortions fuel misleading global narratives. The uncritical repetition of these figures by international media has profoundly shaped public opinion, often to the detriment of truth and justice.

Fox's report highlights four critical issues:

- **Manipulated Casualty Figures:** The MoH inflates death tolls by failing to differentiate between combatants and civilians, over-counting fatalities, and including pre-conflict deaths.
- **Combatant Deaths Omitted:** Only 3 percent of major media reports include combatant fatalities, while 97 percent rely on unverified Hamas figures. This omission reinforces the misleading claim that all deaths are civilian.
- **Hamas Instructions to Mislead:** A 2014 directive instructed operatives to describe all casualties as "innocent civilians" and avoid revealing combatant deaths.
- **Journalistic Failures:** Media outlets' failure to critically evaluate Hamas-supplied data raises significant ethical concerns and risks influencing policy decisions based on misinformation.

## The UNRWA Problem: Hamas Infiltration

The infiltration of UNRWA by Hamas represents another layer of this conflict. Facilities intended for humanitarian purposes have been exploited to store weapons, launch rockets, and embed fighters. Reports from the Coordination of Government Activities in the Territories (COGAT) highlight how Hamas manipulates civilian infrastructure to shield its operations.

This exploitation undermines UNRWA's mission and endangers civilians, yet many media outlets fail to account for this reality when citing UNRWA as a source. By amplifying Hamas narratives without scrutiny, journalists inadvertently legitimise a terrorist organisation while ignoring the true complexity of the situation.

## Journalistic Integrity, Adaptive Campaigning, and Accountability

In the fog of war, journalistic integrity often becomes the first casualty. Many media outlets uncritically echo Hamas's claims, presenting its narratives as fact while casting doubt on Israeli data. By conflating civilian and combatant casualties and disregarding evidence of deliberate manipulation, these reports distort public understanding and embolden terror.

The Australian Army's Adaptive Campaigning framework (now superseded) offered a valuable lens for addressing these challenges. It outlined five interdependent Lines of Operation (LOOs):

- **Joint Land Combat:** Integrating offensive and defensive operations to defeat adversaries
- **Population Protection:** Ensuring the safety of civilians to foster stability

- **Information Actions:** Managing information to counter misinformation and support operational goals
- **Population Support:** Delivering essential services to earn local trust
- **Indigenous Capacity Building:** Strengthening local security forces and governance to sustain peace

The Information Actions LOO remains particularly relevant, stressing the necessity of accurate, verified reporting. Misinformation can mislead audiences, undermine lawful operations, and lend credibility to adversarial propaganda. Upholding journalistic integrity is therefore essential to ensure that information shared during conflicts is truthful and does not inadvertently fuel hostility.

What some Western journalists have done since October 7, 2023, is akin to reproducing propaganda reminiscent of Goebbels' Ministry of Propaganda in the 1940s. The actions of these ideologically compromised journalists range from irresponsible to outright harmful. If a similar dereliction of duty occurred in medicine, those responsible would likely face malpractice lawsuits. The field of journalism must face comparable oversight to restore public confidence in the credibility of what they read and watch.

## A Call to Action

The manipulation of truth in the Gaza conflict is not just an issue for Israel—it is a global problem. The integrity of journalism, the credibility of international organisations, and the ability of nations to counter terrorism are all under threat. To combat this, we must take the following steps:

- **Demand Accountability:** Media outlets must rigorously verify all claims, particularly those from Hamas-controlled sources.
- **Reject Double Standards:** Expose and address selective reporting that applies differing standards to Israel.
- **Demand Integrity:** Governments, institutions, and individuals must challenge falsehoods and print retractions.

Gaslighting and projection are tools of psychological warfare that Hamas has weaponised with devastating effect. As Orwell so aptly warned, "Freedom is the freedom to say that two plus two make four. If that is granted, all else follows."

In this moment of deepening crisis, the world must find the courage to stand for truth, expose falsehoods, and ensure that Israel's efforts to protect innocent lives are recognised for what they are: a defence of justice against a regime that thrives on deception.

# 2

# KEEPING FOCUS ON THE REAL THREAT

## INTRODUCTION

Western societies have become obsessed with manufactured grievances, focusing on ideological debates while ignoring real threats to their survival. This essay argues that the real wolf at the door is not Israel or its policies—it is the global jihadist movement and its enablers in Western institutions.

As radical Islamists openly call for genocide, Western intellectuals and activists focus instead on virtue signalling, political correctness, and identity politics. The result? They fail to confront the genuine threat to their own freedoms and security.

This essay demands a return to moral clarity, urging people to stop being distracted by ideological noise and focus on the actual existential dangers facing the world.

## "EYES ON THE WOLF AT THE DOOR, NOT ON THE LEAK IN THE FLOOR": SIMPLIFYING THE NARRATIVE

*First published in The Australian Jewish News, November 28, 2024*

I recently delivered the keynote address at the Union of Progressive Jews Biennial Conference, held in Canberra, ACT, from November 7–10, 2024. Attendees included members from Australia, New Zealand, and the wider region. It was an honour to be invited into this group, and this article is an adaptation of my speech.

Three main thoughts struck me over the weekend:

1. We are living in a time of profound historical significance. Near the anniversary of Kristallnacht, an actual pogrom occurred in Amsterdam. This event cost me sleep, as I had once believed in the promise of "never again."

2. There is a profound disconnect between the peaceful and kind nature of Jewish people and how they are portrayed by bigots, antisemites, and biased commentators in both social and mainstream media.

3. There is something urgent we can—and must—do to address the growing threat of antisemitism: simplify the narrative and keep our "eyes on the wolf at the door," not "the leak in the floor." The "wolf" is the existential threat, while the "leak" is a nuisance. The "wolf" endangers our children; the "leak" merely irritates those with sensitive toes.

The "wolf" is the Jihadist. For years, Douglas Murray has been clear-eyed about the necessity of acknowledging and confronting explicit threats from such groups. The events in Amsterdam remind us that this isn't a Middle Eastern issue alone—it is a global problem, one that Western democracies must recognise and resolve. The "leak" includes grievances one may hold against leaders like the prime minister of Israel or the president of the United States, which, however valid, cannot distract from the larger threat at hand.

Israel is fighting a war of survival. The Jewish Diaspora is waging a war of information and narrative. Both are critical; both must be won. Israel is winning on the battlefield, but the narrative war is being weakened by internal divisions and trivial disputes.

To illustrate, consider Francesca Albanese, the United Nations Special Rapporteur. She "keeps it simple," and although I find her views reprehensible and baseless, her message gains traction because many non-Jews find her narrative compelling. We must take a page from our adversaries and focus our message on what truly matters: the safety of our children.

To my friends in the Progressive Australian Jewish community, I urge you to help sharpen this focus. Many in the broader community remain blissfully unaware of what happened in Be'eri and Re'im on October 7, 2023, or in Amsterdam on November 7, 2024.

If you are not prepared to help carry this message, please refrain from undermining our efforts.

For those who wish to be part of "the solution," I recommend two recent podcasts:

Amjad Taha, a Muslim expert in strategic political affairs from the United Arab Emirates, discussed the UAE's zero tolerance for antisemitism and terrorism on November 6, 2024.

Ayaan Hirsi Ali spoke with Dan Senor on his *Call Me Back* podcast on November 8, 2024, where she reflected on the pogrom in Amsterdam.

Please search for both episodes using your preferred podcast provider.

I close with words I recently saw in a synagogue: "Pray like everything depends on G-d. Act like everything depends on you."

# 3

# ISRAEL'S CENTURY OF RESILIENCE: 2048 IN RETROSPECT

## INTRODUCTION

This work is a thought experiment. It takes creative liberties, extrapolating from present realities to imagine events that have not—and may never—occur. It is not a prediction, nor a prescription, but rather a lens through which to explore possibilities, challenge prevailing narratives, and question assumptions that shape our understanding of Israel, the West, and the storm that gathers on the horizon.

In crafting this essay, I have deliberately blurred the lines between analysis and fiction, not to deceive, but to illuminate. History is often written in hindsight, its patterns only visible once the chaos has subsided. But what if we could examine today's turbulence through the eyes of tomorrow's historians? What might they say of this moment, of the choices made—or avoided?

This is not an attempt to forecast the future with certainty. It is an exercise in perspective, inspired by the words of Niall Ferguson, who reminds us that "it is difficult to determine the true significance of events as they unfold." In that spirit, I invite you to consider these pages not as a blueprint, but as a challenge—to conventional wisdom, to moral relativism, and to the complacency that too often accompanies the decline of great civilisations.

Whether you agree or disagree with the conclusions drawn, I hope this thought experiment serves its purpose: to provoke, to engage, and to reaffirm that ideas—bold, uncomfortable, and unflinching—still matter in a world where clarity is often sacrificed to convenience.

## A THOUGHT EXPERIMENT

*First published in The Australian Jewish News, February 5, 2025*

We appear to be living in consequential times, marked by upheaval and uncertainty. This article seeks to provide context by taking creative liberties, forecasting future events, and offering a path forward. Written as a thought experiment, it is guided by the wisdom of two enduring observations.

As Lewis Carroll's Cheshire Cat remarked in *Alice's Adventures in Wonderland*, "If you don't know where you are going, any road will get you there." This underscores the importance of intentionality and planning—qualities we must embrace if we are to navigate the complex challenges of our time.

Similarly, as Niall Ferguson observed in *Civilization*, "It is difficult to determine the true significance of events as they unfold, for we are immersed in their chaos and momentum." In this author's view, it is often beneficial to step back from the immediacy of current events and consider how future historians might interpret this era.

## Blue Sky Thinking — Vantage Point of 2048

Reflecting on Israel's enduring resilience, we uncover lessons not only for the Jewish state but for the global community navigating shared crises of confidence. This article offers a simplified framework for forging a better path forward, addressing the intertwined challenges of the Palestinian Territories, Lebanon, Syria, and the broader missteps of Western liberal democracies. By considering how historians in 2048 might interpret the post-October 7, 2023, period, this author aims to chart a course that is both principled and pragmatic—one that honours the wisdom of history while meeting the urgent demands of the future.

## Israel's 100-Year War for Survival: 1948 to 2048

For centuries, the Levant has been synonymous with conflict, yet history demonstrates that peace transforms lives and nations. Treaties like the Abraham Accords have underscored that when Israel and its neighbours embrace diplomacy, the region flourishes economically, culturally, and socially. Today, Israel and the UAE collaborate on groundbreaking initiatives in technology, renewable energy, healthcare, and education, showcasing how partnership can bridge divides and build a brighter future for the region.

The years 2023–2026 marked a pivotal chapter in Israel's "100-Year War for Survival," defined by monumental geopolitical shifts and the permanent decline of Russian and Iranian influence in the region. This transformative period saw the dismantling of violent non-state actors and culminated in historic peace treaties with Lebanon and Syria before 2048, ushering in an era of unprecedented prosperity and collaboration across the Middle East.

These achievements were made possible through sustained punitive sanctions against the Russian Federation and the Islamic Republic of Iran, coupled with decisive actions against terrorist organisations such as Hezbollah and the Muslim Brotherhood. The leadership of these groups was neutralised, their financial networks dismantled, and their ideological influence significantly curtailed.

Aided by US administrations beginning with the 47th President, Israel and the world's Western liberal democracies adopted a "peace through strength" strategy complemented by targeted "maximum pressure campaigns" against destabilising forces. Saudi Arabia's Crown Prince Mohammed bin Salman, alongside other visionary regional leaders, spearheaded a coordinated effort to reshape the future of the Middle East. These initiatives not only redefined the region's political landscape but also laid the foundation for enduring stability and mutual prosperity. Importantly, policy changes did not require the commitment of US forces to the region.

## A New Paradigm for Palestinians

**Resolving Statelessness – Transformative Actions:** By the late 2020s, the long-standing plight of displaced Palestinians was finally addressed through decisive and transformative action. The disestablishment of the United Nations Relief and Works Agency (UNRWA) marked the end of an outdated and ineffective system, with responsibility for Palestinian welfare transitioning to the United Nations High Commissioner for Refugees (UNHCR). This critical shift enabled groundbreaking policies, including granting citizenship to multi-generational

Palestinians, ensuring that those who had resided in Lebanon, Syria, and Jordan for decades became citizens of these respective countries.

Although initially met with resistance from host countries and criticism from activists in Western academia and media, the decision became a turning point. The newly appointed United Nations Secretary-General championed the move:

> "No community can flourish while millions remain stateless for generations. This decision honours the principles of human dignity, sovereignty, and practical necessity. There is no better path forward."

- **Regional Implementation and Economic Gains:** With this long-avoided decision finally taken, Jordan led the way, followed by Lebanon and eventually Syria, each committing substantial resources to integrating their new citizens. These efforts prioritised deradicalisation and counterterrorism, ultimately yielding significant economic benefits and incentive payments from the international community for all three nations. Inspired by the United Arab Emirates' Ministry of Tolerance and Coexistence, these countries established institutions fostering inclusivity and social harmony. The UAE's National Tolerance Programme, launched in 2016, served as a model for promoting mutual respect and peaceful coexistence among diverse communities. By 2048, Lebanon, Syria, and Jordan had adopted similar frameworks, creating opportunities for former refugees to contribute positively, reducing the appeal of extremist ideologies, and enhancing regional stability.

- **Security Infrastructure in Gaza:** Around the Gaza Envelope, an eight-metre-high barrier of concrete T-Walls spanning sixty-five kilometres was constructed, effectively separating Gaza from Israel. As a reforming United Nations Secretary-General optimistically suggested, "the wall is needed now, but can come down later when no longer required."

- **Within the Gaza Envelope:** Territory was divided into D, E, and F zones, each separated by impenetrable barriers guarded by the Israel Defense Forces (IDF). This structured division allowed peaceful communities that renounced terrorism to exist peacefully, free from intimidation and reprisal by irreconcilable remnants of Palestinian terror organisations.

- **Reconstruction, Clearance, and Oversight:** Aid across the Gaza Envelope was coordinated by Israel's Coordination of Government Activities in the Territories (COGAT), with funding partially sourced from the impounded bank accounts of Hamas and Palestinian Authority (PA) leaders, as well as reparations paid to Israel by Qatar and Iran. International aid agencies and the United Nations were granted limited and controlled access, ensuring aid distribution aligned with security priorities.

A critical precondition for progress in Gaza was the comprehensive clearance of Hamas infrastructure, weapons, and rocket caches. This extensive process was pivotal in ensuring long-term security and fostering an environment conducive to peaceful coexistence.

Tragically, not all hostage remains were recoverable and additional IDF and Gazan civilian lives were lost, underscoring the devastating human toll of conflict.

Hamas leaders, who had initially sought sanctuary in Qatar and later Türkiye, were ultimately handed over, extradited to Saudi Arabia, and executed following trial. These actions marked a significant step in dismantling the group's global leadership and operational networks.

- **Governance of Zones D, E, and F:** In Gaza, Zone D was eventually fully administered by local authorities following a decade of IDF supervision and support, marking a step towards local self-governance and stability. Zone E involved joint security coordination between Israel and Abraham Accords partners, ensuring a collaborative approach to maintaining order. Zone F, however, remained under full IDF control to address long-term deradicalisation and stability concerns.

- **In Zone F:** Palestinians continued to reside primarily in temporary tented shelters for several decades. While this drew predictable criticism, particularly from antisemitic factions in Western nations, the United Nations Secretary-General contextualised this situation using data from the UNHCR. By the end of 2023, the total number of forcibly displaced individuals worldwide had reached over 122.6 million, including 32 million refugees under UNHCR's mandate.

The Secretary-General noted that many of these displaced individuals lived in far worse conditions than the 2.2 million Gazans, some of whom remained committed to violent ideologies and activities. The

Secretary-General highlighted that even in these circumstances, the resources and living conditions provided in Gaza's Zone F exceeded those available to many peaceful displaced populations around the globe. Under this balanced perspective, the intergenerational humanitarian aid and support provided by Israel to Palestinians began to be viewed in a more favourable light.

- **Israel's Commitment to Long-Term Security and Presence in Gaza:** Initially unpopular in Israel, the mindset gradually shifted as Israelis recognised that these indispensable elements of national security could not be outsourced to the international community for fear of a "resurrected" UNRWA. The generation of Israelis who fought in Gaza and Lebanon in the aftermath of the October 7 Hamas atrocity collectively resolved to ensure that "this war" in Gaza would be the "last war" in Gaza. In time, this generation came to be known as "Israel's finest generation."

- **Historical Precedents for Sustained Oversight:** The approach of maintaining an indefinite IDF presence in Gaza found precedent in the post-conflict occupations of Germany and Japan following World War II. In both cases, Allied forces remained for decades to oversee reconstruction, ensure security, and prevent the resurgence of extremist ideologies or hostile regimes.

- **Controlling Narratives and Media:** Learning from the 2023–2025 Gaza war—during which international media uncritically echoed Hamas propaganda—Israel implemented stringent measures to control misinformation. International journalists, who often spread falsehoods that went "around the world before the truth puts its pants on," as the famous saying goes, were prevented from accessing the Gaza Envelope. Oversight was provided by the IDF Inspector General, supported by a select team of embedded representatives from Abraham Accords partner nations with oversight by the US Ambassador to Israel. This collaborative arrangement ensured accountability, transparency, and adherence to security protocols while fostering regional cooperation. The United Nations Secretary-General and the US Secretary of State were both frequently briefed.

- **Reforming International Structures:** Francesca Albanese and her organisation, the United Nations Special Rapporteur on the occupied Palestinian territories, long accused of bias and undermining Israel's legitimacy, were defunded and ultimately disbanded. This pivotal action was part of a broader realignment in how the international community approached peace in the region. Recognising the failures of previous frameworks, Western nations, led by the United States and Abraham Accords partners, redirected support towards strengthening Israel's stabilising efforts.

- **Transformations in the West Bank – Governance and Leadership:** In the West Bank—the regions of Judea and Samaria—Western leaders, along with the United Nations Secretary-General, maintained that Israel's presence was necessary until Palestinian leadership capable of fostering coexistence emerged. By the late 2030s, a charismatic leader arose to head the PA after decades of corruption and disappointment. This leader championed reforms, introducing legislation in the Palestinian Legislative Council in Ramallah to outlaw extremist groups like the Muslim Brotherhood, Hamas, and Palestinian Islamic Jihad.

- **Counterterrorism and Reform:** Driven by international pressure, including the withholding of Western funding, significant reforms were implemented to address internal dissent. Palestinian irreconcilables were detained under a model reminiscent of Singapore's post-independence approach, where individuals with incompatible ideologies were incarcerated until renouncing their views. For instance, during Operation Coldstore in 1963, Singapore detained over one hundred leftist leaders and activists without trial to curb communist influence.

- **Innovative Deradicalisation Solutions:** A unique prisoner exchange programme was established, transferring militants from the West Bank to Saudi Arabia in return for advanced Israeli agricultural technology. This arrangement strengthened regional cooperation, discouraged radicalisation among Palestinian youth, and reduced violence against leaders pursuing reconciliation with Israel. While time spent in Israeli prisons is often regarded as a badge of honour, incarceration in Saudi Arabia carries a far more intimidating and deterrent reputation to would-be Palestinian terrorists, amplifying the programme's impact.

- **Peace Without Statehood:** As of 2048, peaceful coexistence had been achieved without Palestinian statehood—an issue that once dominated international discourse but lost urgency after the departure of the Biden Administration in January 2025. While generational challenges remain within the Palestinian diaspora and among antisemitic and social Marxist groups in the Anglosphere, their influence has waned significantly.

Images of thriving Palestinians in Gaza's Zone D and Zone E have become a powerful counter-narrative to extremist 'river to the sea' rhetoric, demonstrating that pragmatic governance and collaboration can achieve lasting peace.

- **Settlements: Rethinking Conventional Approaches:** The notion that a future Palestinian state must be ***Judenrein*** (a term meaning "free of Jews," associated with Nazi-era policies) was widely criticised as both racist and unworkable. Former US Secretary of State John Kerry's approach, which implied the removal of all Jewish communities from Judea and Samaria, faced significant backlash and was discredited by subsequent US administrations and global opinion.

  Israeli communities in Judea and Samaria came to be seen as indispensable for any future Palestinian state. While initial White House narratives "build baby build" were initially seen as unhelpful, the charismatic 48th US President—who earlier served as Vice President—across an eight-year administration effectively messaged that Jewish industry, agriculture, and innovation were essential components for building a sustainable Palestinian economy. This was seconded by the United Nations Secretary-General who recognised the unprecedented opportunity for peace in the middle east that consistent policy and US leadership presented in the aftermath of the October 7 atrocity.

- **Demographics and Integration:** Data from 2025 highlighted Israel's diverse society, with approximately 20 percent of Israelis identifying as Arabs—19 percent Muslim and 1 percent Christian. Drawing from this coexistence, strategists proposed that approximately 15 percent of any future Palestinian state could be Jewish, mirroring Israel's successful integration of Arab citizens. This perspective challenged the traditional narrative of territorial exclusivity, advocating instead for mutual security and economic interdependence.

- **Alternative Frameworks for Peace:** Historical precedents demonstrate that peace can be achieved without statehood through frameworks balancing autonomy, integration, and coexistence. For instance, the Kurdish Region in Iraq functions as an autonomous entity under Iraq's constitution, allowing self-governance and economic development without pursuing full statehood.

- **Second-Order Benefits:** As global attention shifted away from an exclusive focus on Gaza, neglected communities worldwide began to experience renewed support. Refugees in overcrowded camps in Bangladesh, displaced families in the Sahel, and Venezuelan migrants across South America benefited from redirected humanitarian aid and resources.

  Indigenous groups fighting for land rights, stateless populations yearning for recognition, and conflict zones like Yemen and the Tigray region saw fresh energy from international organisations and governments addressing their crises. This broader focus brought a sense of justice and equity to communities long relegated to the shadows.

## Peace Between Lebanon and Israel

Peace between Lebanon and Israel was achieved in the early 2040s, marking a transformative milestone in Middle Eastern diplomacy. The discovery of vast oil and natural gas reserves in the Eastern Mediterranean Sea created an unprecedented opportunity for collaboration. A resource-sharing agreement, brokered with strong US support, allocated 50 percent of the proceeds to Lebanon and 50 percent to Israel, providing a compelling incentive for peace and stability.

This arrangement mirrored Israel's historic 1979 peace treaty with Egypt, in which the return of the Sinai Peninsula became a catalyst for lasting coexistence. Similarly, the resource-sharing agreement fostered mutual prosperity and collaboration, particularly following Hezbollah's eradication as a political and military force:

- **Security and Reconstruction:** The withdrawal of the United Nations Interim Force in Lebanon (UNIFIL) without replacement signified a significant shift in regional security dynamics. Deterrence was maintained through precise Israeli strikes on Hezbollah, effectively preventing its re-establishment south of the Litani River. These operations, sustained for approximately fifteen years after the commencement of the Third Lebanon War (2023-2025), systematically dismantled Hezbollah's operational infrastructure and revenue streams, including its involvement in Lebanon's lucrative drug trade.

- **Asset Seizure:** Simultaneously, a global campaign to seize Hezbollah operatives' assets provided critical funding for the reconstruction of northern Israeli towns such as Metula and Kiryat Shmona, which had suffered severe damage during the hostilities of 2023–2025.
- **Internal Resistance and Shia Cantonments:** The 2030s were marked by intense violence in Lebanon as Hezbollah's stranglehold faced unprecedented resistance. In actions reminiscent of a Dylan Thomas poem—"Do not go gentle into that good night, rage, rage against the dying of the light"—Christian, Druze, and Sunni communities rose up in coordinated efforts to reclaim their autonomy and nation from the tentacles of a resource-deprived and increasingly isolated Hezbollah.

  In response to escalating attacks, Shia cantonments were established to contain the group's dwindling but dangerous influence. These fortified zones aimed to prevent Hezbollah's devastating tactic of choice: suicide attacks targeting civilian and military infrastructure. The conflict represented a turning point, as alliances among Lebanon's diverse communities, coupled with external support, dismantled Hezbollah's grip on the region, paving the way for a fragmented yet more balanced governance structure.

  **Enduring Peace:** In the end, the combination of decisive military action, economic incentives, and strategic isolation created the conditions for the emergence of peace between Lebanon and Israel. The shared prosperity resulting from resource collaboration further strengthened this fragile but enduring peace. In 2048, a limited form of insurgency remained in Lebanon, not dissimilar to that seen in Egypt's Sinai Peninsula in 2025. As Kofi Annan once said, "Peace must be more than the absence of war. It must be nurtured, maintained, and built on foundations of justice, equity, and opportunity."

## Peace Between Syria and Israel

The overthrow of Bashar al-Assad in late 2024 marked a seismic shift in the Middle East. Assad's regime, long synonymous with brutality, corruption, and crimes against humanity, finally collapsed under the weight of internal dissent and external pressures. Russia, preoccupied with its faltering war in Ukraine, and Iran, engaged in direct confrontation with Israel, were unable to sustain the dictator's grip on power.

Assad's atrocities during the Syrian Civil War—including the use of chemical weapons on civilians, mass starvation campaigns in besieged cities, and the torture and murder of thousands in regime prisons—were laid bare to the world in chilling detail. Testimonies from survivors and independent investigations exposed the full scale of his regime's barbarity, solidifying his reputation as one of the twenty-first century's most infamous dictators.

Russia initially offered Assad safe haven, sparking a diplomatic standoff. The International Criminal Court (ICC) and the International Court of Justice (ICJ) played pivotal roles in pursuing justice for Assad's victims. After years of controversy, both institutions revitalised their mandates, focusing on prosecuting egregious crimes and upholding international law.

Spurious charges against Israeli leaders were discontinued, and South Africa was admonished for its earlier stunt at the

ICJ, which had garnered misguided support from countries like Bolivia, Chile, Ireland, and Spain. Meanwhile, Assad and several senior regime officials were handed over for trial, symbolising a renewed global commitment to justice and accountability.

**A New Government and Regional Realignment:** In Syria, the regime that succeeded Assad in 2025—dominated by Hay'at Tahrir al-Sham (HTS), a designated terrorist organisation—initially garnered praise from Western liberal circles as a "revolutionary" force. However, its true nature soon became evident. Under HTS, minorities such as Christians, Druze, and Kurds faced brutal persecution, and Syria's cultural heritage was devastated, with priceless antiquities destroyed.

A generation after Assad's fall, a coalition of moderate opposition leaders, military defectors, and technocrats emerged, gaining broad-based support from Syria's fragmented communities. This government renounced territorial claims over the Golan Heights as a confidence-building measure, paving the way for peace talks with Israel.

In the early 2040s, Syria joined the Abraham Accords, signalling a dramatic realignment in regional diplomacy. Israeli agricultural technology transformed Syria into a regional breadbasket, fostering unprecedented economic growth and lifting millions out of poverty. In 2044, a 79-year-old Bashar al-Assad and his 69-year-old wife Asma al-Assad were both extradited to Syria where they were executed in what many Syrians identified as a necessary moment of catharsis.

Despite modest advances, Syria continues to face an active insurgency, with the Syrian Arab Armed Forces focused on dismantling remnant Sunni and Shia terror cells. In tandem, the secular rulers of Syria and Jordan have intensified efforts to counter violent extremism across the ancient region historically known as Transjordan and the broader Levant.

As Ban Ki-moon once observed, "Peace is not merely the absence of war but the presence of sustainable growth, justice, and hope for all people." Syria's journey towards peace underscores this wisdom, demonstrating that even amidst decades of division, collaboration and determination can create a brighter future for the Middle East.

## Concluding Thoughts: A Century of Survival

History often unfolds in patterns, offering lessons to those with the foresight and courage to act decisively. This thought experiment underscores that the journey to lasting peace and stability, though fraught with challenges, is achievable through resilience, cooperation, and pragmatic solutions. Israel's "100-Year War for Survival" stands as both a cautionary tale and a testament to the enduring power of determination and innovation, proving that even amidst profound adversity, principles of justice and perseverance can lead to transformative outcomes.

Discussions of pragmatic measures—such as prisoner exchanges with Saudi Arabia or the extradition of dictators to face justice in the nations where they committed atrocities—may provoke discomfort for some. Yet, the brutality witnessed on October 7 and the collective suffering of an entire region for centuries demand bold and effective actions. Such steps, however difficult, reflect the gravity of addressing the unchecked spread of extremism and the need to restore dignity and stability to a region long overshadowed by conflict.

As Lewis Carroll's Cheshire Cat reminds us, "If you don't know where you are going, any road will get you there." Israel's survival and eventual flourishing owe much to its clarity of purpose, charting a course that rejected both external pressures and internal despair. The global community, too, must forge paths rooted in equity, pragmatism, and a commitment to long-term stability, eschewing performative activism in favour of substantive change.

Niall Ferguson's insight into the chaos of unfolding events is particularly apt as we reflect on the Middle East's transformative decades. From Lebanon's liberation from Hezbollah to Syria's economic renaissance, these milestones underscore the necessity of deliberate and visionary action. While history's currents may seem overwhelming in the moment, they are ultimately shaped by those willing to act with purpose and conviction. As Eleanor Roosevelt wisely observed, "It isn't enough to talk about peace. One must believe in it. And it isn't enough to believe in it. One must work at it." These lessons from the past century remind us that history is not merely a record of what was—it is a roadmap for what can be.

# 4

# THE MYTH OF JEWISH COLONIALISM: EXPOSING THE HISTORICAL DISTORTIONS

## INTRODUCTION

The claim that Jews are "colonisers" in their own ancestral homeland is one of the most egregious distortions of historical reality. For over 3,000 years, the Jewish people have maintained an unbroken connection to the land of Israel, through both continuous presence and an enduring spiritual, cultural, and historical bond. Despite centuries of exile and persecution, Jewish communities have remained in the land, and those who returned in modern times did so not as imperialists, but as refugees escaping oppression and seeking self-determination.

This essay dismantles the fallacious narrative that seeks to erase Jewish history and falsely equates Jewish nationhood with European colonialism. It examines the historical presence of Jews in the land, the colonial histories of Christianity and Islam, and the modern political weaponisation of anti-Zionist rhetoric. It also highlights how Israel, far from being a colonial project, is the only democracy in the Middle East that upholds religious freedom for all faiths—a stark contrast to the treatment of minorities in many of its neighbouring states.

By exposing the misuse of historical terminology, the failure of academia to challenge ideological bias, and the outright falsehoods propagated in global discourse, this essay reaffirms the incontrovertible truth: The Jewish people are not colonisers. They are the Indigenous people of Israel.

## YOU CANNOT BE SERIOUS

*First published in The Australian Jewish News, January 29, 2025*

### Refuting the Allegation That Jews Are Colonisers

For over 3,000 years, the Jewish people have maintained an unbroken connection to the land now known as Israel. Historical records, archaeological evidence, and religious texts consistently affirm the centrality of this land in Jewish identity and culture. From the ancient Kingdoms of Israel and Judah to the destruction of the First and Second Temples in Jerusalem, Jewish presence has been a defining feature of the region's history. Even during periods of exile and persecution, small Jewish communities endured, safeguarding their ancestral heritage.

Throughout this time, other peoples—including Canaanites, Philistines, Assyrians, Babylonians, Greeks, Romans, Arabs, Crusaders, and Turks—have also inhabited the region. However, their presence often coincided with external empires or transient conquests. Unlike these temporary rulers, the Jewish connection has been deeply spiritual, cultural, and historical. Jews prayed daily for the return to Zion, kept the Hebrew language alive, and maintained a collective memory of their homeland, even in the farthest corners of the Diaspora.

In recent years, however, some academics and activists have sought to distort this historical truth. They allege that modern-day Jews are "colonisers," imposing foreign rule on indigenous Palestinians. This claim is not only ahistorical but reflects a deep-seated bias cloaked in academic jargon. Figures like Ilan Pappé have conveniently ignored the millennia-long Jewish connection to the land and the fact that Jews returned in modern times as refugees fleeing centuries of persecution, not as imperialists. As former US President Joe Biden aptly stated, "You don't have to be a Jew to be a Zionist," affirming that supporting Jewish self-determination in their ancestral homeland is a matter of justice, not imperialism.

## Christianity's Influence in the Land

Christianity, born in the Jewish heartland, spread rapidly after the life and crucifixion of Jesus of Nazareth. The land of Israel became a focal point for Christian pilgrimage and theological reflection. During the Byzantine era, Christian rulers built churches, monasteries, and shrines over sites they deemed holy. Yet, Christianity's influence in the land was often symbolic rather than demographic, as Christian empires came and went.

The Crusades marked a particularly dark chapter. In 1099, Crusaders massacred Jews and Muslims alike in Jerusalem. Despite such atrocities, Jewish communities persisted, though under immense strain. Globally, Christianity's expansion became deeply intertwined with European colonial ambitions. Empires like Spain, Portugal, France, and Britain often used Christianity to justify the conquest and coercion of indigenous populations. Indigenous languages, cultures, and traditions were suppressed under the guise of spreading the Gospel.

Today, Christianity remains a dominant global religion, its enduring reach a legacy of these colonial efforts. However, the story of Christianity in Israel reflects the broader dynamics of empires imposing themselves on the land—a stark contrast to the Jewish people's enduring and organic connection to their homeland.

## The Penetration of Islam

The rise of Islam in the seventh century brought another transformation. Following Arab conquests, the region became part of the Islamic Caliphates, with Jerusalem emerging as a significant religious and political centre. The construction of the Al-Aqsa Mosque and the Dome of the Rock marked the city's importance in Islamic tradition.

Islam's global spread, like Christianity's, was often facilitated through conquest and trade. The concept of Dar al-Islam (House of Islam) and Dar al-Harb (House of War) provided a framework for expanding Islamic governance. While this expansion enriched many societies through trade and scholarship, it often relegated non-Muslims, including Jews, to second-class status as dhimmis. Jews faced discriminatory taxes, restrictions, and periodic violence, such as the 1066 Granada Massacre and the Farhud in Baghdad in 1941.

The 1066 Granada Massacre was a tragic and violent attack on the Jewish community of Granada, in what is now Spain, on December 30, 1066. This massacre resulted in the killing of approximately 4,000 Jews and marked one of the earliest large-scale anti-Jewish pogroms in medieval Islamic Spain.

The Farhud was a violent pogrom, a massacre targeting the Jewish community of Baghdad, Iraq, on June 1 and 2,

1941. The term "Farhud" translates to "violent dispossession" in Arabic. This atrocity occurred during the Jewish festival of Shavuot and is considered one of the most traumatic events in the history of Iraqi Jewry.

Today, political Islam continues to shape the narrative in the region. Groups like Hamas reject Israel's right to exist, intensifying tensions between a radical interpretation of Islamic identity and Jewish self-determination.

## Facts on the Ground

Jerusalem is sacred to Jews, Christians, and Muslims alike and serves as a powerful example of Israel's commitment to religious tolerance. The Temple Mount, known to Muslims as Haram al-Sharif, is home to the Al-Aqsa Mosque and the Dome of the Rock. While Muslims enjoy unrestricted access to these sites, Jewish access is heavily regulated. Israeli authorities enforce limits on Jewish visits and prohibit Jewish prayer at the Mount to prevent tensions with Muslim worshippers.

Under Israeli governance, Jerusalem has seen an unprecedented degree of religious freedom. Holy sites for all faiths, including Christian churches and Baha'i shrines, are protected, and worshippers can practice their religions openly. This policy starkly contrasts with Saudi Arabia's Mecca and Medina, where non-Muslims are forbidden from entering, and no places of worship other than mosques are permitted.

Israel's efforts to preserve Jerusalem as a shared spiritual centre highlight its pluralism. Meanwhile, neighbouring countries such as Syria and Iran impose severe restrictions on religious minorities. For instance, during Christmas 2024, a Christmas tree was burnt in Damascus, reflecting the persecution non-Muslims face across the region.

## The Worst Colonisers in History

If Jews were colonisers, they would be history's least effective. Colonisers exploit land for resources, impose their culture, and subjugate indigenous populations. In contrast, Jews returned to Israel not to conquer but to survive. They revived barren lands, established a thriving democracy, and extended freedoms to minorities unparalleled in the region. Far from erasing other cultures, Israel protects and embraces diversity.

The notion that Jews are colonisers is a dangerous fabrication, reflecting a failure in education and a prioritisation of ideological conformity over historical truth. As Winston Churchill said, "The truth is incontrovertible. Malice may attack it, ignorance may deride it, but in the end, there it is."

## A Note to the Jewish Diaspora

Over the past twelve months, in combating antisemitism and fostering peaceful coexistence, I have realised that reasoning with antisemites is often futile. Their hatred oscillates between irrational and criminal. Such individuals, whether in academia, media, or political activism, must be held accountable under the law.

Yet, there is hope for the uninformed, who lack malice but hold misconceptions. Some are unaware that Israel's population includes 20 percent non-Jews or that Muslim members of the Knesset, such as Mansour Abbas, play integral roles in its democracy. For these individuals, education can be transformative, as "you catch more flies with honey than vinegar."

Our mission is to influence with truth and integrity. In this fight for justice and understanding, let truth be our armour.

# 5

# FALSE EQUIVALENCE: THE REALITY OF ANTISEMITISM VS. ISLAMOPHOBIA

## INTRODUCTION

Antisemitism and Islamophobia are often presented as parallel forms of discrimination, but a closer examination reveals stark differences in their prevalence, impact, and historical roots. While both terms are frequently invoked in public discourse, the reality is that antisemitism manifests with far greater frequency, intensity, and lethality—both in Australia and globally.

This essay provides a comparative analysis of antisemitism and Islamophobia, using data, case studies, and historical context to challenge the false equivalence often drawn between them. It examines the disparity in hate crime statistics, the disproportionate targeting of Jewish communities, and the unique historical trajectory of antisemitism as a systemic and persistent force across centuries.

By exposing the misuse of these terms in media, academia, and political rhetoric, this essay argues that the attempt to equate antisemitism with Islamophobia is misleading and intellectually dishonest. The reality is not even close.

## NOT EVEN CLOSE

*First published in The Australian Jewish News, January 31, 2025*

## A Comparative Analysis of Antisemitism and Islamophobia in Australia and Globally

In recent years, both antisemitism and Islamophobia have garnered significant attention in Australia and worldwide. While both forms of prejudice are deeply concerning, a comparative analysis reveals that antisemitism manifests with greater frequency and severity, both domestically and internationally, particularly when considering the small size of the Jewish population.

## Antisemitism in Australia

The Jewish community in Australia constitutes approximately 91,000 individuals, representing less than 0.4 percent of the total population of nearly 26 million. However, antisemitic incidents are disproportionately high.

The Executive Council of Australian Jewry (ECAJ) documented 495 antisemitic incidents between October 2022 and September 2023, marking a 3.5 percent increase from the previous year. Following the events of October 7, 2023, there was a staggering 316 percent surge in antisemitic incidents, with 2,062 cases recorded in just one month. These incidents included physical assaults, vandalism, and hate speech, disproportionately targeting a tiny minority population. On a per capita basis, this equates to one antisemitic incident for every forty-four Jews in Australia.

## Islamophobia in Australia

The Muslim population in Australia is significantly larger, estimated at approximately 813,000 individuals, or about 3.2 percent of the total population. Islamophobia Register Australia documented 930 verified Islamophobic incidents from 2014 to 2021. Their most recent data shows 133 incidents in a single month following the October 2023 events, compared to the pre-October average of 2.5 incidents per week.

While concerning, the per capita frequency of Islamophobic incidents is significantly lower than that of antisemitic incidents. Even with the surge, this equates to one Islamophobic incident for every 6,100 Muslims during the October–November 2023 period—a stark contrast to the targeting of the Jewish community.

## Acts of Violence in Australia Since October 7, 2023

On October 7, 2023, Hamas militants launched a coordinated attack on Israel, resulting in 1,200 Israeli deaths and numerous abductions. In the aftermath, Australia experienced a significant rise in religiously motivated attacks, exacerbated by the uncritical spread of Hamas propaganda through social media and international outlets. This messaging has amplified hostility, fostering environments conducive to real-world violence.

In April 2024, Bishop Mar Mari Emmanuel—a member of the Assyrian Church of the East, an ancient Christian denomination rooted in Mesopotamia (modern-day Iraq and surrounding regions)—was stabbed during a service at the Christ the Good Shepherd Church in Sydney, losing sight in one eye. The attacker, a sixteen-year-old Muslim, was motivated by religious extremism and inflammatory comments about Islam and the Prophet Muhammad. New South Wales Police classified the incident as a terrorist act.

In November 2024, anti-Israel vandalism and arson in Woollahra, Sydney, led to two arrests. Mohammed Farhat, 20, was detained at Sydney International Airport while attempting to flee to Bali. He faces twenty-one charges, including property destruction, and remains in custody. Thomas Stojanovski, 19, was arrested at his Arncliffe home and faces identical charges. Both await court proceedings.

In December 2024, the Adass Israel Synagogue in Ripponlea, Melbourne, was firebombed. While worshippers escaped unharmed, the attack caused significant damage. Authorities are treating this as a terrorist act and are searching for three suspects.

Later in December 2024, another car arson incident occurred in Woollahra, Sydney. A Toyota Corolla was set ablaze, and anti-Israel graffiti defaced seven properties. Witnesses reported seeing two masked individuals fleeing the scene. The New South Wales Police are investigating the incident as a hate crime.

These incidents underscore the alarming rise in religious tensions, highlighting the need for vigilance and counter-measures against the spread of extremist propaganda. In contrast, there have been no comparable violent crimes targeting Muslims in Australia during this period. While individual cases of Islamophobic rhetoric and minor altercations exist, they do not match the severity or frequency of antisemitic incidents, such as the firebombing of a synagogue or violent physical assaults against Jewish individuals.

## Global Perspective

Globally, the disproportionate nature of antisemitism becomes even more evident when population size is considered:

**United States:** The US, home to approximately 7.5 million Jews (2.3 percent of the population), has seen antisemitic incidents surge by over 200 percent since October 7, 2023, with more than 10,000 cases reported by September 2024. The Anti-Defamation League recorded 400 incidents on college campuses, a stark rise from thirty-three in the same period in 2022, and over 3,000 incidents occurred during anti-Israel rallies, many openly supporting Hamas and Hezbollah. This alarming escalation underscores the growing threat faced by the Jewish community in the US following the Hamas attack on Israel.

**Europe:** Europe, home to significant Jewish populations in France (445,000) and the UK (270,000), has experienced a marked rise in antisemitism since October 7, 2023. In the UK alone, incidents surged by over 500 percent in the weeks following the Hamas attack, compared to the same period in 2022. Many of these incidents occurred alongside anti-Israel protests, often featuring explicit hostility towards Jewish communities. Considering escalating antisemitism and societal tensions in France, Chief Rabbi Haïm Korsia has advised French Jews to consider emigration for their safety. This counsel reflects growing concerns about the community's future amid rising extremism and inadequate protection from political entities. The Chief Rabbi's guidance underscores the precarious position of Jews in France, caught between increasing antizionism on the far left and xenophobia on the far right.

**Globally for Muslims:** Globally, the Muslim population is currently estimated at 1.9 billion, accounting for nearly 25 percent of the world's population. This marks a significant increase from approximately 750 million, or about 16.5 percent of the global population, in 1980. While Islamophobia remains a significant issue, reports indicate that the scale and intensity of targeted violence do not match the per capita prevalence of antisemitic incidents. Nevertheless, numerous Muslim communities face systemic discrimination and societal prejudice, particularly in countries with minority Muslim populations.

## Moral and Legal Obligations

### Religious Teachings on Laws of the Land

The Torah emphasises the principle of "Dina de-Malkhuta Dina" (אָנִיד אָתוּכְלַמְד אָנִיד), meaning "The law of the kingdom is the law," which obligates Jews to follow the civil laws of their host nation, provided they do not conflict with religious commandments.

Similarly, Islamic teachings stress adherence to the laws of the land. The Qur'an states: "O you who have believed, obey Allah and obey the Messenger and those in authority among you." (Surah An-Nisa 4:59). The Prophet Muhammad also taught that agreements and covenants, such as those of citizenship, must be honoured.

### The Australian Values Statement

Australia's approach to promoting social cohesion is embodied in the Australian Values Statement, which visa applicants must sign. Introduced in 2007 as part of changes to the Migration Act 1958, it requires adherence to core Australian values such as respect for the rule of law, equality, and mutual respect. This reflects Australia's commitment to integrating migrants into a society built on democratic and egalitarian principles.

"I confirm that I understand:

Australian society values respect for the freedom and dignity of the individual, freedom of religion, commitment to the rule of law, parliamentary democracy, equality of opportunity for all people, regardless of their race, religion, or ethnic background; and a fair go for all that encourages mutual respect, tolerance, compassion for those in need, and equality of opportunity for all."

I understand that English is Australia's national language and is an important unifying element of Australian society.

I undertake to conduct myself in accordance with these values and to obey the laws of Australia during my stay in Australia."

## Recorded Examples of Religious Clerics Advocating Violence in Australia

A literature review has indicated that within Australia, most religious leaders promote peace and tolerance, yet isolated instances of incendiary rhetoric by clerics from different faiths have drawn attention. These cases, though not representative of broader religious communities, highlight the need for vigilance in addressing divisive rhetoric.

- **Muslim Clerics:** Several Muslim clerics in Australia have faced scrutiny for inflammatory sermons:
    - **Sheikh Feiz Mohammad:** Known for his controversial *Death Series* DVDs, Sheikh Feiz Mohammad has been criticised for urging young Muslims to engage in violent jihad and making derogatory references to Jews, including calling them "pigs." His statements, first reported in 2007, prompted investigations into potential incitement to violence.
    - **Ismail al-Wahwah:** In 2014, Ismail al-Wahwah, a leader of Hizb ut-Tahrir in Australia, called for jihad against Jews, describing them as a "cancerous tumour" to be "uprooted." These remarks were widely condemned for promoting hatred and violence.
    - **Wissam Haddad (Abu Ousayd):** In 2023, Wissam Haddad delivered sermons labelling Jews as "vile" and "treacherous," claiming their influence pervades businesses and the media. Legal action was initiated against him by the Executive Council of Australian Jewry for potential violations of anti-racism laws.
- **Christian Clerics:** While less common, there have been isolated instances of Christian leaders expressing views perceived as inflammatory. Some Protestant preachers have perpetuated the notion that Jews are collectively responsible for the death of Jesus. Although such views are rare, they have been addressed and condemned by both religious and Jewish community organisations.

- **Jewish Clerics:** Incidents involving Jewish clerics (rabbis) in Australia making incendiary statements are extremely rare. In 2012, a rabbi attracted criticism for opposing LGBTQ+ inclusion programmes, arguing that they conflicted with Jewish teachings. While controversial, his stance was framed within religious beliefs rather than promoting violence.

## Antisemitism as a Barometer of Intolerance

Historically, antisemitism has often been described as the "canary in the coal mine," a precursor to broader societal decay. As historian Robert Wistrich aptly stated, "Antisemitism is a light sleeper." Its resurgence serves not merely as an attack on the Jewish people but as a warning sign of rising hatred and societal fragmentation.

In Australia, the disparity between how antisemitic and Islamophobic rhetoric is addressed raises troubling questions. While Jewish communities face a disproportionate share of blame and violence, there is a growing perception that Islamic hate preachers, some of whom skirt the boundaries of incitement, receive less scrutiny or accountability. Addressing these imbalances is critical not only for protecting Jewish communities but for maintaining the integrity of Australia's commitment to justice and equality.

## Conclusion

Both antisemitism and Islamophobia are critical issues requiring attention and action. However, when viewed through the lens of population size and frequency of incidents, antisemitism stands as an unparalleled challenge. In Australia, Jewish individuals are over one hundred times more likely to experience targeted hate than their Muslim counterparts. The stark reality is that, when the data is examined, the disparity is not even close, underscoring the urgent need for focused strategies to combat this form of prejudice.

As historian Yuval Noah Harari has observed, "Data is the most powerful tool we have to understand the world and make informed decisions." Yet, attempts by Australians—whether in parliament, academia, the media, or the wider community—to equate antisemitism and Islamophobia fail to acknowledge these glaring discrepancies. Such comparisons, as critics suggest, "don't pass the pub test." Recognising and addressing these inequities is essential to ensure that resources and policies are targeted appropriately to address the specific challenges faced by each community.

To effectively combat prejudice, policymakers must heed the evidence, allocate resources proportionally, and develop solutions that reflect the unique realities confronting each group. Failure to do so risks diluting efforts to combat hatred and undermining the fundamental values that underpin Australian society.

# HOW THE LEFT BETRAYED ITS OWN IDEALS

## INTRODUCTION

The ideological left once stood for human rights, democracy, and the fight against oppression. Today, it has betrayed those very ideals by aligning itself with Islamist extremists, antisemites, and totalitarian movements.

How did a movement that once championed freedom and equality become apologists for Hamas and Iran? Why do those who claim to stand against fascism march in support of groups that murder women, execute LGBTQ+ individuals, and oppress minorities?

This essay traces the intellectual and moral collapse of the modern left, exposing how it abandoned its principles in favour of ideological purity, identity politics, and anti-Western dogma—regardless of the human cost.

# OF ALL THE TYRANNIES

*First published in The Australian Jewish News, February 18, 2025*

The modern world is witnessing a dangerous conflation of moral absolutism and authoritarianism, a trend disturbingly evident in the Middle East War and the responses it has provoked globally. For those of us who are steadfastly pro-Israel, the stakes are existential, as we grapple with a battle not only for survival but for truth itself. As C.S. Lewis aptly observed in *God in the Dock*: "Of all tyrannies, a tyranny sincerely exercised for the good of its victims may be the most oppressive." This timeless warning resonates today as we confront the insidious rise of social Marxism, the decay of media integrity, and the pervasive threats to individual freedoms.

Lewis's observation cuts to the core of the current predicament. Unlike other forms of tyranny—those driven by greed, power, or corruption—a tyranny imposed under the guise of moral righteousness is relentless. The robber baron may eventually tire or grow sated, but the moral busybody, convinced of their virtue, will persist indefinitely, tormenting with the full weight of their self-assured conscience. This form of tyranny has found fertile ground in the West, where the lunacy of movements like "Queers for Palestine" defies logic, as it champions those who would deny the very freedoms they claim to uphold. Similar contradictions abound, revealing the intellectual bankruptcy of ideologies that prioritise virtue signalling over reason.

## The Middle East War: A Battlefield of Morality and Misinformation

The October 7 atrocities perpetrated by Hamas revealed the brutal reality of Israel's security challenges. 1,200 persons slaughtered in a single day—a deliberate, calculated assault on humanity. Yet, astonishingly, much of the global media equivocated, framing Israel's defensive actions as morally equivalent to the terror it endured. This false equivalence—a hallmark of failed journalism—erodes the moral clarity essential to confronting evil.

As the late British Prime Minister Margaret Thatcher once remarked, "Watch your thoughts, for they will shape your actions; watch your actions, for they will shape your character." The distorted narratives perpetuated by elements of the media and academia have created fertile ground for antisemitism to thrive under the guise of social justice. Calls for "ceasefires" or "proportionality" often mask a deeper bias—one that refuses to recognise the moral chasm between a liberal democracy defending its citizens and a terrorist organisation committed to genocide.

## The Social Marxist Agenda: An Assault on Freedom

Social Marxism refers to the application of Marxist principles beyond economics, extending into cultural and social spheres. Rooted in the ideas of thinkers like Antonio Gramsci and the Frankfurt School, it critiques and seeks to dismantle traditional structures of power, often framing them as systems of oppression. This ideology prioritises identity politics, equity over meritocracy, and the redistribution of cultural and social power to achieve what its proponents see as a more equitable society.

In practice, social Marxism often subordinates individual freedoms and universal principles, such as free speech and due process, to its perceived moral imperative of addressing systemic injustice. Critics argue that it undermines personal responsibility, fosters division, and erodes the foundational values of Western civilisation.

These cultural gatekeepers frequently frame Israel as an imperialist oppressor, ignoring its historical, legal, and moral right to exist. As Thomas Sowell cautioned, "The most basic question is not what is best, but who shall decide what is best." By recasting victimhood as virtue and eroding the principle of universal human rights, social Marxism undermines not just Israel but the very foundations of freedom itself.

## Combatting Antisemitism: Lessons from History

The resurgence of antisemitism in the twenty-first century, particularly in progressive circles, is one of the great paradoxes of our time. While cloaked in the language of human rights, much of this rhetoric is indistinguishable from the old tropes that fuelled centuries of Jewish persecution. As the saying goes, "History doesn't repeat itself, but it often rhymes."

Consider the "anti-Zionist" boycotts, which echo the economic ostracism of Jews in pre-Holocaust Europe. Or the demonisation of Israeli self-defence, reminiscent of medieval blood libels. These modern manifestations of antisemitism are often amplified by social media echo chambers, where outrage is monetised and nuance is sacrificed. The solution lies not only in countering lies with truth but also in fostering genuine dialogue and coexistence.

## Fostering Peaceful Coexistence: A Path Forward

Peaceful coexistence is not a utopian dream but a pragmatic necessity. Israel's story—its achievements in technology, medicine, and agriculture—offers a blueprint for how diverse communities can thrive together. Yet coexistence requires reciprocity, a willingness from all parties to reject hatred and embrace shared humanity.

As the economist and statesman Milton Friedman once noted, "A society that puts equality before freedom will get neither. A society that puts freedom before equality will get a high degree of both." The West's appeasement of radical ideologies, whether in the form of Islamist extremism or its intellectual enablers, only emboldens those who seek to destroy the principles of liberty and coexistence. True peace will emerge not from appeasement but from a firm commitment to justice and truth.

## Failed Media: The Battle for Truth

The role of the media in shaping public opinion cannot be overstated. Unfortunately, much of today's media has abandoned its duty to inform, opting instead for sensationalism and ideological conformity. This failure has dire consequences, particularly in conflicts like the Middle East War, where misinformation can fan the flames of hatred.

Ben Shapiro, a leading conservative thinker, once noted, "Facts don't care about your feelings." Yet the media's obsession with narratives over facts has created a post-truth environment where emotions often trump evidence. The solution lies in rebuilding trust through rigorous journalism, intellectual honesty, and an unwavering commitment to the truth.

## A Call to Action

The challenges we face are immense, but so too is our capacity to overcome them. Combating antisemitism, defending Israel, and fostering peaceful coexistence are not separate battles; they are interconnected fronts in the same war for civilisation. As

Theodore Roosevelt once said, "In any moment of decision, the best thing you can do is the right thing. The worst thing you can do is nothing."

The Jewish Australian community has a unique and pivotal role to play in this struggle. More so than any other part of Australian society, they have witnessed and experienced the malice of social Marxism firsthand. This lived experience gives Jewish Australians a profound understanding of the stakes and the urgency of action. Gentiles and Jews have agency—the ability to influence, to educate, and to lead. Together, we can author a better tomorrow, not only for Australia but for the decaying West as a whole.

The time for action is now. We must stand firm against the tyranny of moral busybodies, the deceit of failed media, and the divisive agenda of social Marxism. By upholding truth, freedom, and justice, we honour the legacy of those who came before us and secure a brighter future for generations to come.

# CONCLUSION TO SECTION III

Not all wars are the same. Some are wars of choice—conflicts fought over politics, territory, or ideology. Others are wars of necessity—existential struggles where survival itself is at stake. Israel has never had the luxury of waging wars of choice; every battle it has fought has been one of necessity.

As Winston Churchill once said, "If you're going through hell, keep going." Israel has endured relentless attacks—on the battlefield and in the court of public opinion—but it has never stopped fighting for its survival.

In the past, wars were won by armies. Today, they are won by those who control the narrative. The war against Israel is not just a military conflict—it is a war over truth, history, and morality. The enemies of Israel do not need to win on the battlefield if they can convince the world to turn against the Jewish state.

This section has revealed how misinformation, media bias, and ideological subversion fuel antisemitism. But understanding the problem is not enough—we must actively fight back.

If we allow lies to become truth, if we accept moral relativism over moral clarity, then the war will be lost before a single bullet is fired.

The question remains: Who will stand for the truth?

SECTION IV

# THE WEST AT A CROSSROADS – THE DECLINE OF MORAL CLARITY

## INTRODUCTION TO SECTION IV

Western civilisation stands at a crossroads.

For decades, the values that defined the West—freedom, democracy, individual rights, and the pursuit of truth—were upheld as the pillars of a just society. Today, these values are under siege from within.

The enemies of Western civilisation are not just external jihadist threats or hostile foreign powers. The greatest danger comes from the ideological decay within the West itself. Universities, media institutions, and political elites have abandoned moral clarity in favour of moral relativism. In their worldview, all cultures are equal, all grievances are valid, and all oppression is interchangeable—even if it means excusing terrorism, justifying antisemitism, and vilifying those who fight for freedom.

Israel's struggle is not just about Israel—it is about the survival of Western values. If the world allows lies, cowardice, and ideological self-destruction to dictate policy, then Western civilisation will not survive the twenty-first century.

This section explores how the West's intellectual and moral decline has enabled antisemitism, empowered totalitarian movements, and placed our future in jeopardy.

# 1

# WHAT HAPPENS WHEN THE WEST ABDICATES ITS RESPONSIBILITIES?

## INTRODUCTION

The greatest fear for Western civilisation is not external invasion—it is internal collapse.

The West was built on a foundation of strength, moral clarity, and the willingness to defend itself. But what happens when Western leaders refuse to confront threats? When the public is conditioned to see weakness as virtue? When cowardice is mistaken for diplomacy?

This essay explores what happens when the West abdicates its responsibilities—how indecision, appeasement, and ideological surrender have emboldened Israel's enemies and weakened the free world.

It asks the critical question: If the West is no longer willing to stand for itself, what will remain?

# THE SUM OF ALL FEARS

*First published in The Australian Jewish News, February 3, 2025*

We live in an era that bears an uncanny resemblance to periods of great upheaval in human history. It is my contention that we are living in an antebellum period—a term derived from the Latin *ante bellum*, meaning "before the war"—a phase marked by tension, division, and the shadow of impending conflict. When historians in 150 years reflect on the first quarter of the twenty-first century, they may observe that the world had already realised two of the four preconditions for a third world war, while the remaining two are partially realised. Rising antisemitism, often a bellwether of societal sickness, is a troubling symptom of the broader malaise afflicting global stability. Drawing upon the insights of Peter Turchin, who argues that cyclical forces drive societies towards conflict, this article explores the geopolitical realities that underscore this unsettling assertion.

## Understanding Antebellum and Historical Cycles

The antebellum period is characterised by a precarious equilibrium, a time when underlying tensions bubble just beneath the surface. Peter Turchin, a scholar of historical dynamics, posits that societies follow predictable cycles of prosperity, stagnation, and conflict. In his work *End Times*, Turchin warns that the world is overdue for a major conflagration, driven by overpopulation, resource scarcity, and elite overproduction—a phenomenon where too many competing elites create instability. While the specific quote, "Periods of prosperity sow the seeds of their own downfall," is a paraphrase, it accurately reflects his theories.

Historical parallels are hard to ignore. The late nineteenth century saw competing empires and the proliferation of militarism culminating in World War I. Similarly, the early twentieth century's unresolved grievances and the rise of totalitarian regimes set the stage for World War II. Today, the conditions of economic uncertainty, political polarisation, and a multi-polar world order echo these antecedents.

## Precondition 1: The Russian Federation and NATO in Ukraine

The first realised precondition is the ongoing conflict between Russia and NATO in Ukraine. This war has its roots in the dissolution of the Soviet Union in 1991, which left Russia grappling with diminished power and influence. Vladimir Putin's vision of restoring Russia's great power status has driven aggressive actions, including the annexation of Crimea in 2014 and the invasion of Ukraine in 2022.

Ukraine represents a flashpoint for Russia's confrontation with the West. NATO's expansion eastward, which Russia perceives as an existential threat, has exacerbated tensions. As Henry Kissinger once noted, "To Russia, Ukraine can never be just a foreign country." The conflict has escalated to a proxy war, with NATO providing military support to Ukraine and Russia intensifying its campaign.

This poses a profound challenge over values for the West. While the eastern Ukrainian provinces of Donetsk and Luhansk maintain cultural and political ties to Russia, if the West abandons developing nations seeking democracy, it may be judged harshly by history. Leaders and diplomats face a delicate balancing act as brinkmanship raises the stakes.

This war is reshaping the global order. Energy markets are disrupted, alliances are tested, and the spectre of nuclear escalation looms large. As Ronald Reagan wisely stated, "Peace is not the absence of conflict; it is the ability to handle conflict by peaceful means." Beyond energy and military implications, the human cost is immense, and the potential for broader regional destabilisation remains a significant threat.

### Precondition 2: Iran and Its Proxies in the Middle East

The second realised precondition is Iran's growing aggression, both directly and through its extensive network of proxies across the Middle East. The Islamic Revolutionary Guard Corps (IRGC) wields significant influence over groups like Hezbollah in Lebanon, the Houthis in Yemen, and various Shia militias in Iraq and Syria. These proxies serve as extensions of Iranian power, destabilising the region and threatening US interests and allies, particularly Israel, Saudi Arabia, and Jordan.

Under Ayatollah Khamenei's leadership, Iran has pursued a strategy of regional hegemony. Its nuclear ambitions and advanced missile programmes exacerbate fears of a broader conflict. The quote "Watch your character; it becomes your destiny," more accurately attributed to Lao Tzu, aptly captures Iran's trajectory of escalating belligerence.

Adding to this regional complexity is Türkiye under Recep Tayyip Erdogan. Erdogan's neo-Ottoman ambitions and authoritarian rule have strained NATO and further destabilised the region. His actions—ranging from suppressing internal dissent to projecting influence in Syria and Libya—have compounded existing challenges.

The region's dynamics are further complicated by the three pillars of violence within Islam: violent Sunni groups that threaten the dynastic monarchy of Saudi Arabia and the secular governance of Egypt, Shia forces led by Iran and Iraq, and the Turkic pillar increasingly shaped by Erdogan's leadership. These groups not only challenge established regimes but also perpetuate a cycle of sectarian violence—commonly referred to as intrareligious or inter-sectarian violence—when Sunni factions attack Shia communities and vice versa. Türkiye's associations with the Muslim Brotherhood exacerbate these tensions and heighten regional instability.

The violence stemming from political Islam, which has raged for approximately fourteen centuries since its inception in the seventh century, continues to challenge the world's democracies and threaten international peace and security. The enduring divides and relentless cycles of conflict—whether sectarian, ideological, or geopolitical—raise an unsettling question: Can a reformation within Islam akin to a Martin Luther or a Renaissance emerge to modernise and soften political Islam? To paraphrase Colin Gray, it appears we are embarking on "another bloody century," or perhaps even millennia, with no discernible end to these persistent cycles of violence.

Amidst this turmoil, Saudi Arabia's Crown Prince Mohammed bin Salman (MBS) has emerged as a pivotal figure. His leadership has introduced significant reforms within the Kingdom, including economic modernisation under the Vision 2030 initiative. Beyond domestic transformation, MBS's rapprochement with Israel and his efforts to normalise relations between the two nations offer a glimpse of hope for a more stable Middle East. If successful, his initiatives could signal a historic turning point, although these ambitions remain fraught with challenges posed by internal dissent and external threats.

There are perhaps five persons on the planet at any one time who are truly indispensable. In my judgement, Mohammed bin Salman is one of them. His vision and leadership carry profound implications, not only for Saudi Arabia but for the future stability and peace of the Middle East.

## *Precondition 3: Structural Weaknesses in Western Democracies*

One of the most significant yet underappreciated partially realised preconditions threatening global stability is the growing structural weaknesses within Western democracies. These vulnerabilities span economic, demographic, ideological, and cultural domains, each compounding the other:

**Energy Policies and Dependence:** Energy policies prioritising ideological goals over pragmatism have left many nations vulnerable to energy crises. Over-reliance on renewable energy sources without adequate backups, compounded by ongoing reliance on Russian gas during the early stages of the Ukraine war, exposed critical weaknesses in European energy strategies. Former US Energy Secretary Ernest Moniz captured this succinctly: "Energy security remains the cornerstone of national security."

**Demographic Challenges:** Declining birth rates across the West, coupled with aging populations, have strained social welfare systems. Margaret Thatcher's observation, "The problem with socialism is that eventually, you run out of other people's money," resonates in this context. Societies failing to reproduce face existential challenges, highlighting the role of family and societal respect for motherhood. While I support reproductive choice, societies that fail to prioritise family structures risk demographic collapse.

**Elite Overproduction:** Historian Niall Ferguson's concept of "elite overproduction" warns of the societal stagnation created by an overabundance of elites pursuing degrees with limited practical application. Disillusionment among graduates unable to secure meaningful roles fuels unrest and dissatisfaction. Governments must reassess how public funds are allocated in tertiary education, prioritising fields that advance societal benefit. Universities promoting anti-Western ideologies must face consequences, including deregistration, with faculty redirected to experience firsthand the societies they idealise.

**Immigration and Integration:** Immigration policies in many Western nations have compounded social tensions. Cultural incompatibilities and inadequate integration efforts have fostered unrest in countries such as Sweden, Belgium, and the UK. Critics argue that neo-Marxist ideologies dominating political discourse undermine national identity. Former Senator Jim Webb remarked, "A nation without borders is not a nation," underscoring the need for cohesive immigration policies. Assimilation—once seen as a necessity—is now dismissed, a trend that must change for societies to thrive.

**A Crisis of Values:** Western democracies are increasingly distracted by ideological causes that undermine societal cohesion and strategic focus. Intersectionality, environmentalism, and the erosion of Judeo-Christian values have diverted attention from existential threats. Samuel Huntington's *The Clash of Civilizations* warns that cultural and ideological divisions can destabilise societies as much as external adversaries. Angela Merkel's refugee policies and Barack Obama's international strategies, once lauded, are now critiqued for exacerbating geopolitical and domestic instability. Leading from behind, as Obama famously articulated, is no strategy at all—it is capitulation.

**Our Failed Fourth Estate:** The role of the media as the fourth estate has diminished. Legacy media outlets often fail to critique left-of-centre policies with the same rigour applied to others. George Orwell aptly stated, "Journalism is printing what someone else does not want published; everything else is public relations." This dereliction of duty has eroded public trust, leaving voters ill-equipped to make informed decisions.

In my reading of history, societies do not die of old age; they commit suicide. Western democracies must confront these internal challenges. As Abraham Lincoln warned, "A house divided against itself cannot stand." The internal discord within the West, driven by polarisation and the erosion of shared cultural values, presents vulnerabilities that adversaries will inevitably exploit.

## Precondition 4: Chinese Adventurism in the Western Pacific

The fourth precondition, still unrealised, is the growing threat posed by Chinese adventurism in the Western Pacific. Since Deng Xiaoping's reforms in the 1970s, China has risen as a global power. Deng's pragmatic approach—"It doesn't matter if a cat is black or white as long as it catches mice"—enabled economic growth while maintaining totalitarian control. However, under Xi Jinping, China has become increasingly assertive, challenging the post-World War II liberal order.

Xi's "Chinese Dream," rooted in the traditional "Middle Kingdom" mindset, envisions China as the global hegemon. Beijing's territorial claims in the South China Sea, aggressive rhetoric towards Taiwan, and military modernisation underscore these ambitions. Japan's recent declaration that Taiwan's security is integral to its own survival and its rearmament efforts highlight the stakes.

China faces significant internal challenges, including a declining population projected to shrink dramatically by 2100 and structural economic issues such as an overleveraged property market. These pressures strain the social contract that has underpinned the Communist Party's rule: economic growth in exchange for political acquiescence. Kevin Rudd and Rush Doshi have extensively analysed Xi Jinping's leadership, highlighting his adherence to Marxist-Leninist nationalism and a strategic vision aimed at displacing American dominance. Rudd underscores Xi's ideological framework as one rooted in centralised political control and assertive foreign policy, while Doshi details China's systematic approach to achieving regional and global hegemony. Both scholars emphasise Xi's use of nationalism as a powerful tool to consolidate domestic control and advance China's ambitions.

This author is concerned that Xi may follow the "dictator's playbook," exploiting nationalism and manufacturing external conflicts to divert attention from domestic mismanagement by the Chinese Communist Party (CCP) and his growing unpopularity. Likely targets for scapegoating include India, Japan, or the United States, given their strategic significance and existing tensions with Beijing. In such a scenario, external scapegoating could serve to unite the populace and reinforce the regime's grip on power, with potentially grave consequences for regional and global stability.

Adding to this volatile mix is North Korea, whose provocations, including missile tests and nuclear threats, serve as a destabilising wildcard. Kim Jong-un's opportunism heightens regional tensions and could draw major powers into conflict.

## A Period of Historical Significance

We are living in a period of historical significance, where the choices we make will determine the trajectory of global stability. As Ronald Reagan warned, "Freedom is never more than one generation away from extinction." The challenge of the twenty-first century is to avert global conflict and forge a new paradigm of cooperation and resilience.

## We Have Agency

While the challenges ahead are formidable, history has shown that humanity can rise above division to confront shared threats. Albert Einstein's wisdom, "If I had an hour to solve a problem, I'd spend 55 minutes thinking about the problem and 5 minutes thinking about solutions," emphasises the need for thoughtful, deliberate action:

- **Elections Have Consequences:** In this era of significance, elections appear more consequential than at any other time in my lived history. We must exercise our agency wisely.
- **Appeasement Doesn't Work:** History demonstrates that appeasement emboldens aggressors. Choices must carry consequences.
- **Maximum Pressure Campaigns:** Sanctions should be maintained, strengthened, or imposed against regimes like North Korea, Iran, and Qatar. Türkiye's NATO membership should be reconsidered, with sanctions applied where necessary. Qatar's ties to Hamas and

extremist ideologies must be addressed, including relocating the US airbase to the UAE.

- **Peace Through Strength:** As the Roman adage states, "If you want peace, prepare for war." Strong defence postures deter aggression and enable meaningful diplomacy.
- **Stick to Our Values:** Franklin D. Roosevelt's assertion, "The only thing we have to fear is fear itself," reminds us to remain steadfast in our principles despite difficulties.
- **F*^k Around and Find Out:** In an age where the world's challenges exceed the ability of the developed world to resolve, it is reasonable and prudent for certain behaviours to be expected of a nation-state or non-state actor(s). Misbehaviour must attract consequences. As the Chinese adage—"Kill the chicken to scare the monkey"—advises, clear and decisive actions against transgressors serve as a warning to others, reinforcing the importance of accountability in maintaining global stability.

## Conclusion

While the future may seem daunting, history reminds us that even in the darkest times, humanity has risen to meet great challenges. The currents of instability described here—preconditions for what could spiral into *The Sum of All Fears*—are not inevitable outcomes but warnings. They compel us to act with purpose, resolve, and unity.

As the founder and CEO of a harm-minimisation charity combating antisemitism, I believe that Jews in the diaspora—in partnership with gentiles of right mind—have a pivotal role to play in addressing these preconditions. The Jewish people, guided by a heritage of resilience and a commitment to justice, are uniquely placed to foster dialogue, bridge divides, and inspire solutions. It's time for our light to shine, illuminating a path forward amid the shadows of uncertainty.

By confronting these challenges collectively and decisively, we can defuse the tensions that threaten to consume us and lay the foundations for a brighter, more stable future. This is not a task for one group or nation but a shared responsibility for all who value peace and the preservation of civilisation.

# 2

# PONDERING THE UNTHINKABLE – WHAT IT WOULD MEAN FOR THE WORLD

## INTRODUCTION

The survival of Israel is the survival of Western civilisation.

Israel is not just another country—it is the front line of democracy in a region dominated by authoritarianism, theocracy, and tyranny. If Israel were to fall, it would not just be a tragedy for the Jewish people—it would signal the death of Western resolve.

If Israel falls, who will defend democracy in the Middle East?

If Israel falls, who will stop jihadist expansionism?

If Israel falls, what does it mean for the future of the West?

This essay examines the global consequences of Israel's destruction—and why its survival is a non-negotiable necessity for the free world.

## SHOULD ISRAEL FALL

*First published in The Australian Jewish News, January 30, 2025*

I was deeply moved and quite horrified by a recent speech delivered by Ronald S. Lauder, President of the World Jewish Congress, at the eightieth anniversary of the liberation of Auschwitz. Aspects of Lauder's speech where he referred to the Holocaust and the pogrom of October 7, 2023, were incredibly powerful and poignant. When he referred to the apparent sentiment of large proportions of our young, it caused me to lose sleep:

"Almost half of young Americans believe that Israel has no right to exist…no right to exist…. And they are our future leaders…. This is happening in every single country represented here today…"

The fact that this did not dominate front pages across the Western world is a damning indictment—not only of the media but of the leaders who sat silently in the audience, including the King of England, the French President, and Australia's Foreign Minister. It also shows how far we have fallen in eighty years, while survivors of the Holocaust, as infants or young children, continue to draw breath.

The fall of Israel is not just a possibility entertained by its enemies—it is a scenario that, if realised, would shake the foundations of global stability. The world is dangerously unprepared for what comes next. This article explores the unthinkable: what may happen should Israel fall.

I believe that many of those who loudly profess anti-Israel sentiments—such as the individuals referenced above—have invested little to no serious thought into the matter. In fact, the strength of their convictions seems inversely proportional to the depth of their understanding.

It is my judgement that seven second-order effects would occur if Israel were to fall.

## 1 — An Actual Genocide

Forget the ill-informed and the antisemites across Australian universities, chanting slander in our public places, and the many who frequent the Australian Broadcasting Corporation (ABC) and other failed legacy media. They have been droning on about Gaza for well over a year. There never was a genocide in Gaza, but there would be in Israel should she fall.

Israel is home to over seven million Jews. Where would they go? Under the current Australian federal government, Jews are not safe in Australia. South Africa under the African National Congress? Hardly a refuge. In France, the Chief Rabbi recently warned of rising antisemitism and even recommended that Jews consider leaving. Ireland? The virulent hatred displayed in recent times rules it out.

That leaves the United States, under its 47th President, who in a matter of weeks has shown greater and more consistent support for Israel than at any time since January 2021. But even in America, Jewish students are being assaulted on college campuses, and antisemitism is on the rise. The grim reality is that there is no haven should Israel fall.

Hamas leaders have openly called for genocide. On October 24, 2023, senior Hamas official Ghazi Hamad declared, "Israel is a country that has no place on our land. We must remove that country." Iran's Supreme Leader Ayatollah Khamenei has referred to Israel as a "cancerous tumour" that must be "cut out."

Also, without Israel, there is no safe place for women and minorities in the Middle East—Christians, Druze, Bahá'í, Circassians, and the LGBTQ+ community would face persecution, exile, or extermination. Israel remains the only refuge in the region where these groups can live with dignity and full rights, something its detractors conveniently ignore.

This is something the scandalously and misleadingly named Jewish Council of Australia and the dolts in the Queers for Palestine movement should reflect upon.

## 2 — A Crisis of Confidence in the Failed United States Alliance System

The US-Israel military and strategic relationship is one of the strongest in the world. Israel is America's most reliable ally in the Middle East, providing critical intelligence, technological innovations, and military capabilities. If Israel were to fall, confidence in America's commitments to its allies would be irreparably damaged.

If Israel falls, it would not be the first time the United States has failed to protect an ally under siege. The rapid fall of South Vietnam in 1975, the chaotic withdrawal from Afghanistan in 2021, and the failure to deter Russia from invading Ukraine despite security assurances all prove one thing: America's allies cannot afford blind faith in its promises.

Countries like Taiwan, Japan, and Poland would be forced to rethink their reliance on American support. The implications are as dire as they are unpredictable.

## 3 — A Crisis of Confidence in the Most Productive 0.2 Percent on the Planet

Jews make up just 0.2 percent of the world's population, yet their contributions to humanity are immeasurable. In medicine, Jews have pioneered vaccines and lifesaving treatments. In science, they have won Nobel Prizes at a rate exponentially higher than any other group. In commerce, they have shaped global finance and industry.

Israel is not just a refuge for Jews—it is an irreplaceable global hub of innovation. It leads in cyber technology, water desalination, AI, and medical research. A world without Israel would be a world with fewer medical breakthroughs, weaker cybersecurity, and diminished innovation.

Maslow had a few things to say about human requirements. Self-actualisation requires certain prerequisites, such as a reasonable degree of confidence that your children will be safe on the way to and while at school. If the most productive 0.2 percent of human beings on the planet turn their attention exclusively to survival—and away from the arts, science, commerce, and human betterment—the whole human race suffers.

## 4 — Loss of Intelligence Sharing on Jihadists

Israel plays an essential role in global counterterrorism. Its intelligence services have foiled countless jihadist attacks worldwide, including in Australia and the UK. Without Israel, Western nations would be blind to many threats.

The types of terrorists who murdered Lee Rigby on the streets of London, or who planned attacks in Sydney and Melbourne, would find it a whole lot easier to operate. The intelligence Israel provides would dry up, leaving the West exposed to increased terrorism.

## 5 — Opportunism by Rogue Regimes and Elements

Mike Kelly coined the term "rectangle of ratbags" to describe Russia, China, Iran, and North Korea. Should Israel fall, these regimes could be expected to operate opportunistically and seek to expand their influence.

As Western credibility collapses, rogue regimes will not hesitate to act. Iran will not stop at conventional warfare; the nuclear race in the Middle East will begin in earnest.

Meanwhile, transnational terrorist groups like Hamas, Hezbollah, ISIS, Al-Qaeda, and the Houthis would be emboldened, creating widespread instability and wrecking global trade. One could expect a return of the Barbary Pirates across the Mediterranean from North Africa much as we are seeing now in the Red Sea, where the Houthis are actively targeting commercial shipping.

## 6 — Probable Nuclearisation and the Risk of Nuclear Miscalculation

Iran would likely seize the moment to become a nuclear power. This would almost certainly trigger a nuclear arms race in the Middle East, with Saudi Arabia and Egypt seeking nuclear capabilities as a counterbalance.

In Asia, Japan has long debated whether to develop nuclear weapons in response to regional threats. A senior Japanese official recently stated that Japan would need only a matter of months to build a bomb if necessary.

If Israel were to fall, the world would become a much more dangerous place, teetering on the edge of nuclear catastrophe.

## 7 — Rage Against the Dying of the Light

Let's rewind a few steps. If any reader believes that the Jewish State will respond with anything less than the full force of a Dylan Thomas poem—more creatively, intelligently, and entirely—then they have not been paying attention. Since October 7, 2023, this fight has been existential—not just for Israel, but for the Jewish Diaspora globally.

Dylan Thomas wrote "Do Not Go Gentle into That Good Night" in 1947 as a defiant ode to his dying father, urging him to resist the inevitable with every fibre of his being. It is a poem about resilience, about refusing to surrender in the face of darkness. Israel today embodies that same spirit—it will not go gentle into that good night. It will rage, fight, and endure, for surrender is not an option, and defeat is unthinkable.

I am not Jewish, yet I see this reality as clearly as the keyboard upon which I type. Israel will fight—and Israel will win. But should it find itself on the brink, there will be, in my judgement, not a single means or munition left untried or unexpended including its nuclear arsenal. History has proven that when Israel's existence is threatened, it does not capitulate—it prevails. And it will do so again, no matter the cost.

## In Aggregate: Another Dark Age?

The fall of Israel would not be an isolated event—it could trigger a broader collapse of global stability, plunging much of the world into chaos reminiscent of the Dark Ages. The assumption that humanity is on an unbroken trajectory of progress is a dangerous delusion.

Civilisation is fragile, and history provides no guarantees of forward momentum. The great empires of antiquity—Rome, Byzantium, and Persia—once seemed indomitable, yet each succumbed to internal decay and external aggression. The notion that the modern West is immune to such decline is wishful thinking at best, suicidal hubris at worst.

Historically, revolutions have a way of consuming their own. The anarchists and radicals now rallying against Israel, convinced of their moral superiority, may soon find themselves among the first casualties of the lawlessness and barbarism they have helped unleash.

The French Revolution devoured Robespierre and its architects; the Bolshevik purges turned on their own initiators. Trotsky, the architect of the Red Army, was hunted down and murdered in exile. Those who stoke the flames of disorder often fail to realise that fire does not discriminate.

Should Western civilisation deteriorate, the ideologues who dream of utopian destruction will confront a bitter truth—one akin to leaping from a plane without a parachute, only grasping their folly moments before impact.

## The Jihadists' Greater Ambition: After the Little Satan, the Big Satan, Then the Rest of Us

But does it end there? No.

The jihadists who seek Israel's annihilation, aided and abetted by complicit antisemites and hard-left zealots in the West, have other designs. In their worldview, Israel is merely the little Satan—a stepping stone towards their greater ambition.

Ayatollah Khomeini declared in 1979:

> "We shall export our revolution throughout
> the world... until the calls of 'There is no god
> but Allah' resound over the whole world."

The destruction of Israel, they believe, is only a precursor to the fall of the big Satan—the United States and, by extension, Western civilisation itself. This is not speculation; it is doctrine.

Iran's regime has been consistent in its rhetoric for over four decades. Since 1979, Iranian leaders—from Khomeini to Khamenei, from Ahmadinejad to Raisi—have openly and consistently called for Israel's destruction. This is not political posturing; it is an ideological obsession, enshrined in their revolutionary ethos and backed by their actions through proxy groups like Hezbollah, Hamas, and the Houthis.

And let's be clear—Israel is not the only target. The crosshairs extend to Saudi Arabia, the Gulf States, and beyond. The secular rulers of Egypt, which sits astride the critical Suez Canal, are also marked for removal in the Islamist vision of a regional caliphate.

Whether people like to admit it or not, our way of life still depends on petrochemicals, and nothing good will happen if the Middle East descends into true chaos and anarchy. The price of oil, global trade, and strategic supply chains all hinge on some level of stability in the region.

If Iran and its terror proxies succeed in toppling Israel, do Western progressives think Saudi Arabia, the UAE, or Egypt will be left untouched? Do they truly believe that Europe, already struggling with the consequences of mass migration and energy dependence, would remain insulated from the shockwaves?

And before anyone suggests that the world can simply "transition" to a utopian green energy future during such upheaval, a reality check is in order.

There is no amount of screeching from Greta Thunberg, no furious gaze into a TikTok camera, that will change the fact that modern civilisation still runs on oil, gas, and hard geopolitical realities.

Tip for young players: If you find yourself on the same side of a debate as Greta, you may be doing something wrong.

As the world teeters on the brink, now is not the time for self-indulgent fantasies—it is a time for hard-headed realism.

## A Call to Action

History does not wait for the hesitant. This is a moment for clarity, courage, and action. Those who value civilisation must take a stand—before it is too late.

## What Are We Teaching Our Young?

That so many educated people across Western nations have been indoctrinated into anti-Israel sentiment is a shameful indictment of our education systems, media, and common sense. Social Marxists—those who have applied Marxist class struggle to cultural and social issues, seeking to dismantle traditional values, national identities, and institutions—appear to have infiltrated academia, media, and political institutions. In doing so, they have subverted truth, replacing it with a radical agenda aimed at eroding Western civilisation from within.

This ideological subversion has produced a generation that mindlessly parrots anti-Israel propaganda without grasping its implications. As Ronald Lauder warns, "Education—serious, honest education—is the only way to correct this, and that won't be easy. Entire institutions will have to be overhauled and reformed. And that goes for the media as well." The fight against antisemitism is not just about defending Israel—it is about preserving the principles of truth, reason, and moral clarity that uphold Western civilisation itself.

The Chinese proverb "Kill the chicken to scare the monkey" underscores the necessity of making an example of one wrongdoer to deter others. This principle of deterrence must be applied not only to those who promote antisemitism under the guise of activism but also to those who abdicate leadership and decision-making when decisive action is required. Mark Scott (no relation) should not remain at Sydney University. If he possessed any decency or capacity for self-reflection, he would have already resigned.

Academics who support the Boycott, Divestment, and Sanctions (BDS) movement—an insidious campaign aimed at the economic, cultural, and political isolation of Israel—should not be entrusted with educating our youth. Universities that harbour such individuals must remove them from their positions and strip them of their influence over the next generation. Likewise, Australian union members who spew antisemitic taunts should be expelled without hesitation.

Failure to act decisively against these agents of hatred only emboldens them further. The message must be clear: Tolerance of intolerance is not virtue—it is complicity.

## But What About the Palestinians?

"But what about the Palestinians?"—this is the reflexive reframe frequently thrown at anyone seriously attempting to discuss Israel with those whose perspectives have been shaped by "opinion" masquerading as journalism, particularly from broadcasters like the ABC. So, let's talk about the Palestinians. And yes, having lived in Israel and travelled extensively, I have many Palestinian friends. I have seen their reality firsthand, and I refuse to indulge in the naive, surface-level narratives pushed by Western media and campus activists who have never set foot in the region.

There is a truism: Perfection does not exist in nature. In a perfect world, would I like to see the creation of a Palestinian state? Yes, of course. But that is simply impossible and perhaps will be for more than twenty years—if not indefinitely.

Palestinian Authority (PA) terrorism, Hamas's entrenched influence, and residual capabilities in the West Bank make this abundantly clear. The PA has demonstrated time and again that it is incapable of self-government, plagued by repression, economic mismanagement, and security failures that make statehood a dangerous proposition.

Moreover, the Palestinians have shown no collective desire to live in peace with their Jewish neighbours. Instead of extending a hand in peaceful coexistence, they have chosen to fight, kill, and destroy. Why is this? Because for decades, they have been rewarded for their misbehaviour. Every act of terror, every incitement to violence, every rejection of peace has been met not with consequences, but with rivers of gold—international sympathy, diplomatic indulgence, and massive financial aid, much of which is siphoned off by corrupt leadership.

Every evil action seems to result in another round of Israel-bashing, another UN resolution, another influx of foreign cash. But this game appears to be ending. This decades-long charade has run its course.

Despite the incompetence of John Kerry in the Obama administration—who consistently prioritised Palestinian grievances over broader regional stability—the Abraham Accords shattered the long-held assumption that no Arab state would normalise relations with Israel without first resolving the Palestinian issue. The accords, signed by Israel, the United Arab Emirates, Bahrain, Morocco, and Sudan, demonstrated that pragmatic Arab nations had grown tired of Palestinian intransigence and their repeated failures to seize historic opportunities. It is my assessment that this growing realisation—that the world was moving on—helped trigger the October 7, 2023, pogrom. Hamas understood that the Palestinian cause was slipping into irrelevance and sought to change the narrative through barbaric violence. Tragically, many in the West gobbled up the propaganda like catnip, willingly playing into the hands of those who orchestrated the bloodshed.

Despite receiving billions in international aid, the Palestinian economy remains stagnant, with funds frequently misappropriated by PA officials rather than invested in infrastructure or the well-being of the population. This is not Israel's doing. Transparency International has consistently ranked the PA as one of the most corrupt governing bodies in the region. Human rights abuses are rampant—journalists, activists, and political opponents are routinely arrested, tortured, or even killed, as seen in the brutal 2021 murder of Nizar Banat, a prominent PA critic beaten to death by security forces. Such authoritarian practices are the hallmark of a failed leadership, not a viable state.

Security is another glaring issue. The PA's inability to prevent terror attacks, crack down on armed militias, or even control its own territory demonstrates its incompetence. In

Jenin and Nablus, PA security forces have all but lost control to Iran-backed terror groups, while Hamas steadily increases its influence in the West Bank. Mahmoud Abbas, now in his nineteenth year of a four-year term, has clung to power without elections, ensuring that any future Palestinian state would be just another failed dictatorship. Given this reality, calls for an immediate Palestinian state are not just naive—they are dangerously irresponsible.

We don't live in a perfect world, and the world can very much live without a Palestinian state.

Or should we say—another Palestinian state? Jordan, on the East Bank of the River Jordan, is home to millions of Palestinians. With approximately 70 percent of its population being Palestinian, Jordan is, in effect, already a Palestinian state—though ruled by the Hashemite monarchy, a dynasty originating from the Arabian Peninsula. Jordan is not a terror state, but it is a monarchical dictatorship ruled with an iron fist, where the King maintains absolute authority over government, security forces, and political expression. Yet, despite this reality, the world continues to push for the creation of a second Palestinian state, one that, given the current leadership and conditions, would almost certainly become another failed, destabilising entity.

Can the world live without Israel? No. Israel and the United States of America are, in my judgement, the world's only indispensable countries. While neither is perfect—no nation is— they are, at their core, societies built on decency, democracy, and moral clarity. They serve as beacons of light in what could otherwise be an abyss of tyranny and chaos. Any academics or agitators who claim otherwise should be supported in their one-way journey to one of their so-called fools' paradises in the

Middle East or any of the totalitarian states currently seeking to dismantle the rules-based global order. Reality, after all, has a way of correcting delusions.

## Be Careful What You Wish For

To those who wish for Israel's downfall, I say this: Be careful what you wish for. The consequences would be catastrophic—not just for Israel, but for the world.

A quote I saw in the immediate aftermath of October 7, 2023, was both prescient and painfully accurate: "If you ever stopped to wonder what you would have done if you'd lived in Europe in the 1930s, I have news for you: You're doing it now." Too many people, whether through ignorance or malice, are aligning themselves with the same forces of hatred and destruction that history has already condemned.

If you find yourself debating whether my words are too harsh, if you catch yourself dissecting seven different angles before forming an opinion—shame on you. Find a mirror, stare into it, and recognise who the problem is in Western society in 2025. The fact that you can distract yourself with thoughts of whether I am right or simply lacking nuance means you are the problem. You are no different from the hand-wringing enablers of the 1930s—those who rationalised, intellectualised, and excused evil while it gathered strength. Some of them, no doubt, were regretful after the fact. But when it mattered most, they were worse than useless. They were complicit. If you are hesitating in your support for Israel now, you are that person.

Perhaps my concern for the safety and future of my children is no greater than that of the ignoramuses screaming, "From the river to the sea, Palestine will be free." But there is one critical difference: For thirty years, as a professional soldier in the Australian Army, I have seen firsthand the fragility of civilisation, the horrors of unchecked violence, and the grim realities of the human condition. I call on my fellow Australians to examine their unconscious biases and acknowledge that the antisemitism festering in our streets and institutions is nothing more than grotesque Jew-hatred cloaked in moral posturing.

This is why, in 2023, I founded The 2023 Foundation—a harm-minimisation charity dedicated to combating antisemitism and fostering peaceful coexistence. We cannot afford to be passive observers of history repeating itself. The future is not predetermined, and history does not have to repeat itself. But that may depend entirely on whether we choose to act now.

I, for one, will not be a bystander.

# 3

# HOW THE WEST HAS ENABLED TERRORISM

## INTRODUCTION

The Middle East has long been a theatre of competing interests, historical grievances, and strategic miscalculations. However, the policies of recent US administrations—particularly those of Barack Obama and Joe Biden—have contributed to a dangerous legacy of instability. What was once a region governed by clear alliances and deterrence strategies has, in recent years, become more unpredictable, with adversaries like Iran, Hamas, Hezbollah, and the Houthis emboldened by policy missteps and diplomatic naivety.

This essay examines the consequences of key American foreign policy decisions, from the Iran nuclear deal to the reversal of sanctions on terrorist entities and the withholding of military support for Israel at critical moments. It explores how strategic errors, miscalculations, and ideological shifts within the US Democratic Party have led to a deterioration of regional security, an alienation of traditional allies, and an emboldened Iranian regime.

By analysing these developments, this essay argues that rather than fostering peace and stability, these policies have sown chaos, rewarded bad actors, and weakened the very alliances that once upheld regional order. The 2024 election shift among Jewish American voters, previously a staunch Democratic bloc, signals a growing awareness of these failures and the need for a reassessment of Western engagement in the Middle East.

## A LEGACY OF INSTABILITY

*First published in The Australian Jewish News, January 22, 2025*

The Middle East has long been a theatre of complex politics, historical grievances, and competing interests. Many observers may lack familiarity with the intricacies of Middle East policy, which makes the backlash among some staunch US Democrat voters against the policies of Barack Obama and Joe Biden particularly striking. Previously, an overwhelming majority of Jewish Americans had been steadfast supporters of the Democratic candidate, whoever that may have been. That changed in November 2024. Data suggests this shift was not merely a matter of domestic politics but a response to decisions with profound implications for the Middle East and the Jewish diaspora.

This article seeks to shed light on this informed exodus by examining key policy decisions, deviations from previous administrations, and their far-reaching consequences. While evaluating the full impact of Obama's and Biden's approaches in such a volatile region will require the passage of time, certain prima facie observations suggest their Middle Eastern policies may ultimately be remembered for amplifying instability, emboldening adversaries, and weakening alliances.

## Iran: A Tale of Missteps and Consequences

The Joint Comprehensive Plan of Action (JCPOA), commonly known as the Iran Nuclear Deal, was the Obama administration's signature foreign policy initiative. Finalised in 2015, the agreement was reached between Iran and the P5+1 nations (the United States, the United Kingdom, France, Russia, China, and Germany), with the European Union acting as a mediator. The JCPOA aimed to restrict Iran's nuclear programme to ensure it remained exclusively peaceful. In exchange, international sanctions on Iran were lifted, granting the country access to billions of dollars in frozen assets and global markets.

Key provisions of the agreement included limiting uranium enrichment to 3.67 percent, capping Iran's stockpile of enriched uranium, and reducing the number of centrifuges it could operate. Additionally, the deal established a rigorous inspection regime under the International Atomic Energy Agency (IAEA) to verify Iran's compliance. While supporters heralded the agreement as a diplomatic achievement that delayed Iran's potential path to nuclear weaponisation, critics identified significant shortcomings. They argued the JCPOA failed to address Iran's ballistic missile programme, regional aggression, and support for militant proxies. Furthermore, the financial relief provided to Tehran was seen as enabling its destabilising activities throughout the Middle East.

The agreement faced intense backlash, particularly from Israel and Saudi Arabia—two of Iran's most immediate and impacted neighbours, and key allies of the United States. Israeli and Saudi leaders criticised the deal for overlooking critical elements of Iran's regional behaviour. They warned that the billions of dollars unfrozen under the agreement would flow to

Iran's Revolutionary Guard Corps (IRGC) and directly fund its proxies, including Hezbollah, Hamas, and the Houthis. These groups have long played central roles in regional destabilisation, often targeting Saudi and Israeli interests.

While the JCPOA temporarily curtailed Iran's nuclear enrichment activities, it did little to mitigate its broader aggression in the Middle East. Israeli leaders argued that the deal legitimised Iran's nuclear ambitions without dismantling its future capacity to weaponise. Meanwhile, Saudi Arabia highlighted how the agreement failed to address Iran's sponsorship of terrorism and destabilising interventions in Syria, Yemen, Lebanon, and Iraq. Both nations viewed the JCPOA as entrenching Tehran's influence and emboldening its aggressive behaviour.

During the Biden administration, loosened sanctions further exacerbated these concerns. By 2023, Iran's oil exports surged, generating $44 billion in annual revenue. China, purchasing over 1.2 million barrels per day, was a primary beneficiary, while other recipients included Syria, Venezuela, and clandestine Russian markets. This influx of cash not only bolstered Tehran's economy but also empowered its military ambitions and emboldened its proxies, amplifying tensions across the region. Reports from the Foundation for Defense of Democracies and the International Atomic Energy Agency corroborated these troubling trends, painting a stark picture of the unintended consequences of policies designed to constrain Iran.

## Houthi Sanctions: A Reversal with Consequences

In January 2021, just days before President Trump left office, his administration designated the Houthis as a Foreign Terrorist Organization (FTO). This move aimed to curb Iranian-backed aggression in Yemen, protect critical maritime routes, and disrupt the Houthis' financing. The comprehensive sanctions froze assets, restricted financial transactions, and targeted Houthi leaders, effectively cutting off significant revenue streams and limiting the group's operational capacity.

However, President Biden reversed this decision upon assuming office, citing humanitarian concerns about impeding aid to Yemeni civilians. While perhaps well-intentioned, this policy change emboldened the Houthis. In 2021 alone, they launched over 375 drone and missile strikes on Saudi Arabia, targeting oil facilities and civilian areas. These attacks disrupted global energy markets, leading to price increases in economies like Australia and further straining the post-pandemic recovery. Maritime security in the Bab el-Mandeb Strait—a vital chokepoint for global trade—remained under constant threat.

By February 2022, facing mounting criticism, the Biden administration reimposed partial sanctions on the Houthis. However, these were notably weaker and more targeted than the original FTO designation. Critics argued that these concessions were part of a broader effort to revive the JCPOA with Iran. Bolstered by Iranian support, the Houthis intensified their aggression, further destabilising global energy markets and threatening international security. As late as January 2025, the US military was conducting kinetic strikes on this terrorist organisation to mitigate its growing threat.

## Withholding Weapons from Israel

The aftermath of Hamas's October 7, 2023, attack on Israel, which claimed 1,200 civilian lives, demanded unequivocal support from allies. Yet, the Biden administration delayed the delivery of critical munitions, citing logistical challenges and concerns over escalation. This hesitancy drew widespread criticism and was seen by some as indicative of wavering resolve.

Former US Ambassador to the United Nations Nikki Haley stated, "When a nation like Israel is under attack, any delay in military aid sends a dangerous signal to its enemies. This is a moment for solidarity, not hesitation." Former Israeli Defense Minister Yoav Gallant similarly lamented, "Withholding weapons during a time of war ties one hand behind Israel's back while emboldening our adversaries."

## Direct Attacks by Iran on Israel

Iran's aggression towards Israel has escalated beyond its proxies, with Tehran directly targeting Israeli military and civilian infrastructure. In 2024, Iran launched two significant attacks on Israel from Iranian territory.

The first, in April, involved a massive assault featuring over 300 drones, ballistic missiles, and cruise missiles aimed at various Israeli assets, including a naval vessel in the Red Sea. Despite Israel's robust defence systems, damage was inflicted, marking the most aggressive direct action by Iran in recent history.

The second, in October, saw approximately 180 ballistic missiles launched towards Israel. This assault resulted in casualties and material damage. These attacks employed some of Iran's most advanced weaponry, including the Fateh-313 missile, which boasts a destructive radius of up to 500 metres (twenty-five to thirty-five city blocks in Paris). Such sustained aggression underscored Tehran's growing willingness to escalate directly against Israel.

It is impossible to imagine any other first-world nation not responding decisively to such a brazen assault. Yet, this was the pressure the Biden administration levelled on Israel, with

President Biden urging Israeli leaders to "take the win" rather than retaliate.

Israel's unparalleled four-layer missile defence system—Iron Dome, David's Sling, Arrow 2, and Arrow 3—once again demonstrated extraordinary ingenuity in foiling sustained attacks. Few nations possess such comprehensive defensive capabilities. However, this technological prowess seems to contribute to a broader international immaturity in understanding Israel's plight.

I am forming the view that the political elite and, perhaps, the public in many Western nations appear to view Israel's ability to mitigate existential threats as an expectation rather than a remarkable feat, undermining empathy for the nation's unique and precarious security challenges.

The international community appears to have become the proverbial "slow-boiled frog," acclimatising to escalating threats against Israel without recognising their broader implications. If missiles with the destructive capabilities of the Fateh-313 were fired at London, Paris, Sydney, Auckland, or Los Angeles, the global response would likely be swift and unequivocal. Yet, when such attacks target Israel, muted outrage and calls for restraint often replace support.

Richard Goldberg, a senior adviser at the Foundation for Defense of Democracies, remarked, "Iran's escalation in 2024 is the direct result of policies that signal indecision and a lack of resolve. Tehran views the absence of a strong deterrent as an invitation to test the limits of Israeli and international tolerance."

## From Stalemate to Solutions to Subsequent Missteps

John Kerry, as Secretary of State under President Obama, was a central figure in crafting US policy towards the Israeli-Palestinian conflict. His approach rested heavily on the long-standing assumption that peace in the Middle East hinged on resolving the Israeli-Palestinian issue. The Obama Administration's efforts culminated in a high-profile push for peace talks in 2013–2014, but his strategy—emphasising preconditions and harshly critiquing Israeli policies—yielded no tangible results. In stark contrast, the Trump administration's Abraham Accords reshaped the regional landscape, bypassing the Palestinian issue to foster unprecedented cooperation between Israel and several Arab nations.

The Obama Administration's approach was rooted in a belief that Israeli settlement expansion was the primary obstacle to peace. Kerry's public rebukes of Israel alienated its leadership, with Prime Minister Benjamin Netanyahu calling his criticism "obsessive and unbalanced." Kerry's infamous 2016 speech asserted that "there will be no separate peace between Israel and the Arab world without the Palestinian process," dismissing any possibility of broader regional diplomacy. This rigid stance ignored the evolving priorities of Arab nations, particularly their growing alignment with Israel on countering Iranian aggression.

The Obama Administration's fixation on the Israeli-Palestinian conflict as a prerequisite for peace ignored emerging opportunities for collaboration between Israel and Arab states. His insistence on preconditions, coupled with his administration's backing of UN Resolution 2334—which was adopted on December 23, 2016, after Donald Trump had won the US presidential election in November but before he took office in January 2017—which condemned Israeli settlements, further strained US-Israel relations without bringing the Palestinians closer to the negotiating table.

In contrast, the Trump administration rejected the Obama administration's framework and pursued a pragmatic, interest-driven approach to Middle East diplomacy. The result was the Abraham Accords, a series of historic agreements signed in 2020 between Israel and the United Arab Emirates, Bahrain, Sudan, and Morocco. The accords normalised diplomatic, economic, and security relations between Israel and these Arab nations, marking a dramatic shift in the region's dynamics. Key terms of the Abraham Accords included the following:

- **Normalisation of Relations:** Establishment of full diplomatic ties, including embassies and direct flights
- **Economic Cooperation:** Agreements on trade, innovation, and energy projects, such as Israel's solar energy collaboration with the UAE
- **Security Partnerships:** Enhanced intelligence-sharing and joint military training to counter shared threats like Iran

Under the Biden administration, there has been a noticeable regression in the momentum generated by the Abraham Accords. While Biden has expressed lukewarm support for the accords, his administration has deprioritised their expansion, focusing instead on reviving failed frameworks tied to the Palestinian issue. Critics argued that this shift has discouraged further breakthroughs, particularly with Saudi Arabia, which was reportedly close to joining the accords during Trump's presidency.

Saudi Arabia's inclusion would have been a monumental achievement, solidifying a regional coalition against Iran and creating a broader framework for Middle East stability. Former US Ambassador to Israel David Friedman remarked, "We were on the cusp of bringing Saudi Arabia into the fold. What was missing was sustained U.S. leadership to bridge the final gaps." Biden's return to Obama-era priorities, including re-engaging with Iran and downplaying the Abraham Accords, has been described by commentators as a "strategic blunder."

## Possible Reasons and Implications for Australia

A significant shift in US Democratic Party policies towards the radical left has created divisions within its traditional support base. Obama-era intersectional policies—which critics argue prioritised divisive identity politics over unifying principles—alienated many long-standing supporters. This shift, exacerbated by Biden's perceived alignment with progressive radicals, has left some Jewish Americans questioning their place in the party.

Prominent voices have described this as "pandering to the radical left." Former Democratic strategist Mark Penn noted, "The Democratic Party's sharp turn toward intersectionality risks alienating core supporters. Loyalty is a two-way street." Jewish Americans, many of whom have been lifelong Democratic voters, now face the reality that their loyalty was not reciprocated.

Parallels to Australian politics are striking. The exodus of Jewish Americans from the Democratic Party, driven by perceived abandonment during critical moments, serves as a stark warning of what happens when parties—whether that be the Australian Labor Party (ALP) or the Teal 'Independents'—take their Australian Jewish base for granted.

## Mea Culpa

In my thirty-year military career, I have maintained political awareness but a strictly apolitical approach. I now, however, affirm that in 2008, I desired an Obama win. In part, this was due to concerns over John McCain's age and the prospect of a Sarah Palin presidency. Additionally, I was weary after eight years of neo-conservative policies and captivated by the charm and spell cast by Obama.

Even in 2016, when I believed a Clinton presidency was the better prospect, I remained unaware of the magnitude and implications of Obama's policy missteps as they related to the Middle East. At the time, I found myself sceptical of Prime Minister Benjamin Netanyahu's warnings about Iran, influenced by prominent voices suggesting his concerns were exaggerated. For instance, former Mossad chief Meir Dagan dismissed Netanyahu's alarmism and consideration of taking unilateral action as "the stupidest thing I have ever heard," while Uzi Eilam, a retired brigadier general, accused Netanyahu of exploiting the Iranian threat for political objectives. In retrospect, many of Netanyahu's warnings about the limitations of the JCPOA and the broader risks posed by Iran's regional ambitions have been validated.

It was not until the Trump presidency, with its Maximum Pressure Campaign against Iran and the emergence of the Abraham Accords, that I truly "awoke." I awoke to the threat Iran posed not just to the region but to the international rules-based global order. Israeli and Saudi Arabian leaders had been right all along in their opposition to Obama's policies and their reimplementation under Biden. I know of no historical precedent where showering repressive regimes with financial windfalls resulted in their transformation into democracies. Expecting an autocratic regime to develop an inner "Thomas Jefferson" is naive at best and catastrophically misguided at worst.

## How May History Judge?

As Barbara Tuchman observed, "Policy errors are not always immediately apparent, but time exposes their consequences." While the full impact of the Obama and Biden Middle Eastern policies remains to be seen, initial assessments suggest a legacy marked by appeasement, hesitation, and missed opportunities.

Some critics argue that these policies reflect the most significant missteps in US Middle Eastern strategy since the Carter administration—perhaps worse. This is not simply naivety; history may eventually judge the Obama and Biden missteps as malfeasance. Their decisions—from emboldening Iran to undermining Israeli security—seem less accidental and more indicative of a deliberate strategy prioritising diplomatic optics over substantive stability. This did not go unnoticed by Jewish Americans who previously were lifelong Democrats.

## Conclusion

The Middle East remains one of the world's most complex regions, which in my judgement requires leadership that prioritises strength, accountability, and the fostering of alliances. While Obama's and Biden's policies may have aimed for diplomacy, their legacy—at least for now—appears to be one of heightened instability and weakened trust among allies. Future administrations must learn from these lessons and adopt policies that combine firm resolve with a clear-eyed understanding of regional dynamics.

4

# HOW WEAK LEADERSHIP ENDANGERS ISRAEL AND THE WEST

## INTRODUCTION

Leadership at the United Nations requires moral clarity, impartiality, and the ability to mediate conflicts without bias. António Guterres, who assumed the role of UN Secretary-General in 2017, was expected to bring pragmatism and diplomacy to an institution often mired in bureaucracy and ideological division. Instead, his tenure has been marked by a failure to uphold the UN's founding principles, selective application of international law, and a reluctance to confront the world's most pressing security threats with consistency.

Nowhere is this more evident than in his handling of the Israeli-Palestinian conflict. While previous UN leaders, such as Kofi Annan and Ban Ki-moon, maintained at least a degree of diplomatic balance, Guterres has presided over an era where the UN's credibility as a neutral mediator has further eroded. His failure to hold groups like Hamas and Hezbollah accountable, his reluctance to condemn state-sponsored terrorism, and his disregard for Israel's legitimate security concerns raise critical questions about his leadership and the UN's broader role in global affairs.

This essay examines Guterres's approach to Israel, his broader diplomatic record, and the structural failures of the UN under his leadership. By comparing his tenure to that of his predecessors and analysing key geopolitical events, this piece argues that his leadership has not only weakened the UN but also emboldened its most dangerous actors.

## ANATOMY OF A FAILED LEADER

_First published in The Australian Jewish News, January 19, 2025_

## Introduction

António Guterres, the United Nations Secretary-General since January 2017, assumed office with a reputation for pragmatism and diplomacy. As a former Prime Minister of Portugal (1995–2002) and UN High Commissioner for Refugees (2005–2015), Guterres was celebrated for his empathetic leadership. However, his tenure as Secretary-General has been marred by accusations of ineffectiveness, bias, and a failure to address pressing global crises with impartiality.

This article examines Guterres's leadership, focusing on his approach to Israel and its broader implications for the credibility of the United Nations.

## The Role of the United Nations Secretary-General

The United Nations Secretary-General serves as the chief administrative officer of the UN and a global advocate for peace, as outlined in Chapter XV of the UN Charter. Responsibilities include overseeing the UN Secretariat, managing resources and staff, and ensuring the effective implementation of policies and programmes. The Secretary-General employs their "good offices" to mediate conflicts, foster dialogue, and promote peaceful resolutions. Under Article 99 of the Charter, they can also draw the Security Council's attention to threats to international peace and security.

In addition to diplomacy, the Secretary-General serves as a public advocate, articulating the collective concerns of member states and representing the UN at high-profile events. Tasked with upholding principles of sovereignty, equality, and justice, the Secretary-General's influence relies heavily on moral authority and cooperation from member states. This often leaves them constrained by geopolitical dynamics, particularly by the Permanent Members of the Security Council.

## Guterres's Record with Israel

The UN Charter, particularly Chapter VI, emphasises peaceful conflict resolution through negotiation and mediation. Articles 33–38 outline mechanisms for preventing conflict, but Guterres's tenure reveals selective application of these principles.

A historical parallel illustrates these challenges. Prior to the 1967 Six-Day War, Egyptian President Gamal Abdel Nasser demanded the withdrawal of the United Nations Emergency Force (UNEF) from the Sinai Peninsula. Bound by provisions requiring host-nation consent for peacekeeping missions, UNEF complied, leaving Israel vulnerable to an attack by a coalition of Arab armies.

In late 2024, Israeli Prime Minister Benjamin Netanyahu requested the withdrawal of UN peacekeepers from southern Lebanon, citing Hezbollah's militarisation near UN bases. Guterres rejected the request, arguing that the UN's presence was vital for stability. Critics in Israel accused him of shielding Hezbollah and obstructing Israeli efforts to neutralise the threat.

This inconsistency exemplifies the challenges Israel faces within the UN framework under Guterres's leadership: In 1967, withdrawal facilitated aggression; in 2024, refusal to withdraw emboldened a terrorist organisation.

## Comparing Leadership: Ban Ki-moon and Kofi Annan

Guterres's predecessors demonstrated a more balanced approach to Israel and broader international issues. Ban Ki-moon, who served as Secretary-General from 2007 to 2016, publicly condemned Hamas for using human shields during conflicts and consistently defended Israel's right to self-defence. His measured criticisms of Israeli policies were tempered by recognition of its security needs, earning him a degree of respect from Israeli leaders.

Similarly, Kofi Annan (1997–2006) voiced criticisms of Israel at times but balanced them by emphasising Israel's right to secure and recognised borders. Annan's tenure was marked by efforts to mediate in the Middle East, and his leadership was seen as reflective of the UN's founding principles of fairness and impartiality.

By contrast, Guterres has often appeared hesitant to criticise groups like Hezbollah or Hamas, even when their actions flagrantly violate international law. This perceived partiality has eroded trust in his leadership and undermined the UN's credibility as a neutral mediator.

## Guterres's Relationship with Yasser Arafat

António Guterres's engagement with Yasser Arafat, Chairman of the Palestine Liberation Organization (PLO), provides insight into his approach to Middle Eastern conflicts. As a socialist leader in Portugal during the 1990s, Guterres maintained a visible relationship with Arafat, who sought international legitimacy while oscillating between diplomacy and terrorism.

Guterres frequently affirmed the PLO's aspirations for statehood but rarely condemned its complicity in violence. Critics argue that this history has influenced Guterres's tenure as Secretary-General, contributing to a perceived reluctance to hold groups like Hamas accountable, even when their actions flagrantly violate international law.

## Broader Criticism of Guterres

António Guterres's tenure has faced widespread criticism for perceived shortcomings in his advocacy and response to global crises. While he does not command military forces, his role as a moral and diplomatic leader requires effective advocacy for those suffering under oppression and conflict.

- **Rohingya Crisis:** In 2017, Myanmar's military displaced over 700,000 Rohingya Muslims. While Guterres condemned the violence as "ethnic cleansing," his inability to galvanise international action left the Rohingya in prolonged vulnerability.
- **Syrian Civil War:** The Syrian conflict, ongoing since 2011, has caused massive humanitarian suffering. Guterres's efforts to advance political settlements and humanitarian aid have been widely seen as ineffective.
- **Russian Invasion of Ukraine:** Russia's full-scale invasion in February 2022 presented one of the gravest threats to international peace since World War II.

Guterres's delayed condemnation and limited diplomatic impact were criticised as inadequate.

- **Nagorno-Karabakh Conflict:** Escalations in 2020 and 2023 highlighted the UN's limited role in mediating disputes. Guterres's response was confined to statements urging restraint, failing to prevent ethnic cleansing or secure peace.
- **Afghanistan's Fall to the Taliban:** After the US withdrawal in 2021, the Taliban regained control, triggering widespread human rights abuses. Guterres expressed solidarity with Afghan civilians but was criticised for lacking a coherent strategy to protect vulnerable populations.

While Guterres has often spoken against atrocities, critics contend that his leadership has failed to leverage the moral authority of his office to drive meaningful action.

## An Unwanted Title

While Guterres faces substantial criticism, Kurt Waldheim (1972–1981) is often cited as the "worst-ever Secretary-General." Waldheim's tenure was overshadowed by revelations of his Nazi-era affiliations and perceived failures in addressing apartheid and Middle East conflicts.

Although Guterres lacks similar personal controversies, his perceived ineffectiveness and bias risk placing him alongside Waldheim in the annals of UN history.

## A Vision for the Future

The challenges facing the United Nations are significant but not insurmountable. Historical precedents illustrate the potential for institutions to evolve and grow stronger through reform. Together, the United Nations and its predecessor, the failed League of Nations, are only 105 years old.

In Europe, the journey from the Magna Carta (1215) to the Treaty of Westphalia (1648) spanned centuries. The Magna Carta laid the foundation for the rule of law, limiting arbitrary authority, while the Treaty of Westphalia established the principles of national sovereignty and non-interference, shaping modern international relations. These milestones were not instantaneous but emerged through persistent efforts to address systemic failures and conflicts.

China's history offers another example of institutional evolution. The consolidation of the Middle Kingdom under the Qin Dynasty (221–206 BCE) unified warring states and standardised systems of governance, language, and currency. This unification was further refined during the Tang (618–907 CE) and Song (960–1279 CE) Dynasties, which promoted economic prosperity, technological innovation, and administrative sophistication. Such progress highlights the necessity of long-term commitment to reform and stability.

For the United Nations, these lessons are clear. Institutional maturation requires a commitment to restoring credibility, adopting thrift in operations, and embracing incremental improvements. By focusing on fairness, accountability, and tangible results, the UN can rebuild trust and adapt to the challenges of the twenty-first century.

## Conclusion

By objective measures, Guterres to date has not been a successful or effective Secretary-General. He has not reached the standards of his predecessors, Kofi Annan or Ban Ki-moon, though time will tell if he stoops far enough to threaten Kurt Waldheim for an unwanted title.

It is my assessment that the United Nations is an indispensable institution. It is better to have a forum for nation-states to articulate and debate vexed matters than not to have one at all. However, the UN is at a critical juncture, as it is not fit for purpose and is in dire need of reform.

Bold action is required to restore its credibility and ensure that it remains a force for peace and progress. This is likely to necessitate new leadership, replacing the Secretary-General, and a thorough overhaul of the upper echelons of UN departments and agencies. Donor nations should consider withholding funding until meaningful reforms are implemented, guided by clear and measurable key performance indicators.

As Albert Einstein observed, "We cannot solve our problems with the same thinking we used when we created them." This applies to the UN, which must rethink its operational models to overcome inefficiencies and redundancies. A significant reduction in staff numbers and a focus on streamlining processes will be essential to improving its effectiveness.

With principled leadership and committed member states, the UN can transform its weaknesses into strengths and emerge as a beacon of hope, justice, and cooperation in an increasingly divided world.

Failure to act risks relegating the UN to irrelevance, a relic of an earlier era unable to meet the demands of a complex and interconnected global community. Reform is not merely an option; it is an imperative for the survival and success of the organisation.

# 5

# HOW INTERNATIONAL POLICIES ENDANGERED ISRAEL

## INTRODUCTION

The October 7, 2023, attack on Israel by Hamas was not just an act of unprecedented brutality; it was the culmination of years of dangerous policies, international pressures, and strategic miscalculations that left Israel exposed. While the immediate perpetrators were Hamas terrorists, their ability to strike with such devastating precision was, in part, enabled by external actors—foreign governments, international organisations, and ideological movements—that undermined Israel's security posture under the guise of diplomacy and human rights advocacy.

This essay examines the role of global narratives, UN interventions, and misguided diplomatic pressures that contributed to Israel's vulnerabilities leading up to the attack. It argues that while Israel must undertake a full internal review of its own security lapses, the broader international community must also reckon with its share of the blame for enabling an environment where Israel was pressured to take security risks that ultimately proved fatal.

As history has repeatedly shown, prioritising optics over security is a deadly miscalculation. The events of October 7 serve as a grim reminder that appeasement does not deter those committed to destruction—and that Israel's survival cannot be subject to the moral posturing of an international community that has consistently failed to grasp the realities of its existence.

## A SHARE OF THE BLAME

_First published in The Australian Jewish News, January 13, 2025_

## Introduction

The October 7, 2023, attack on Israel by Hamas exposed the stark divide in global reactions. For those with a functioning moral compass, the calculated brutality and devastating impact were shocking and unequivocally condemned. Appallingly, however, others applauded the savagery, blamed the victims, and justified the atrocities as a response to Israel's existence. Beyond the immediate horrors, systemic vulnerabilities and unheeded warnings contributed to the tragedy. Among these factors was the influence of international criticism—voiced by prominent leaders, the United Nations, and international organisations—which, in my assessment, undermined critical security measures and created weaknesses ruthlessly exploited by Hamas.

The purpose of this article is to examine the external pressures and narratives that contributed to the weakening of Israel's defences, resulting in one of the most devastating days in its history. It aims to highlight the dangerous consequences of compromising security for political optics, challenge the misguided narratives that have shaped global discourse, and call for greater accountability among international actors whose actions and rhetoric exacerbated Israel's vulnerabilities.

## An Inquiry Awaits

Israel is expected to conduct a comprehensive inquiry akin to the Winograd Commission following the 2006 Lebanon War. Accountability will likely extend to senior officials, including the defence minister, Israel Defense Forces (IDF) chief, southern commander, and intelligence leaders, with ultimate responsibility resting on the prime minister. While internal failures will rightly be scrutinised, this article focuses on external pressures from foreign leaders and transnational organisations. These external actors, while likely evading formal scrutiny, in my judgement, bear a share of the blame for creating an environment that encouraged detrimental policy shifts and exposed critical vulnerabilities.

## The Security Barrier

Humanity often succumbs to the delusion that barriers, once built, are impenetrable. History proves otherwise. The Maginot Line, France's vaunted defensive system against Germany, was bypassed in 1940 when German forces invaded through Belgium. Similarly, Israel's Bar Lev Line along the Suez Canal was breached during the 1973 Yom Kippur War when Egyptian forces ingeniously used water cannons to erode its sand berms. These examples starkly illustrate the limitations of static defences against determined and adaptive adversaries.

Yet, something had to be constructed between the peace-desiring citizens of southern Israel and the psychopaths in Hamas, scheming for Israel's destruction mere metres from

Israeli population centres. With neighbouring Egypt and Jordan steadfastly refusing to integrate Gaza's population, Israel had no choice but to erect the most robust barrier that international scrutiny would permit.

Stretching approximately sixty-five kilometres from Kerem Shalom Kibbutz near the Egyptian border to Zikim Kibbutz on the Mediterranean coast, the Gaza security barrier was a multi-layered defence. Below ground, it comprised a concrete wall tens of metres—exact depth is sensitive—deep, equipped with advanced sensors to detect tunnelling, specifically countering Hamas's use of subterranean infiltration. Above ground, a steel barrier added an additional layer of protection. Built at an estimated cost of $1.1 billion, the barrier became a cornerstone of Israel's defence strategy, bolstered by cameras, sensors, and optics in an attempt to provide protection at reduced personnel costs.

Despite its necessity, the barrier faced relentless international criticism. United Nations Secretary-General António Guterres described Gaza as "a living hell for millions." Former UK Labour Party leader Jeremy Corbyn called it an "open-air prison," condemning Israel's measures as "collective punishment." Shimon Peres countered these narratives, stating, "We must be vigilant, for our survival depends on it." Richard Kemp added, "Israel's security measures are a response to threats, not a cause of them."

## Retrospective Coherence

Compromising security in the hope of achieving a better tomorrow is a perilous gamble, and history offers little evidence that concessions to adversaries yield enduring goodwill. This misguided notion shaped both the design of the Gaza barrier and subsequent policies that created critical vulnerabilities.

The Gaza barrier's steel structure contrasts starkly with the robust West Bank barrier. Designed to prevent terror attacks during the Second Intifada, the West Bank barrier features prefabricated concrete walls up to eight metres (twenty-six feet) high, trenches, and electronic fences. This barrier successfully reduced attacks originating from the West Bank by over 90 percent, yet it faced global condemnation, with critics labelling it a "wall of segregation."

As John F. Kennedy once said of the Berlin Wall, "A wall is better than a war." In Israel's case, a stronger Gaza barrier might have averted the massacre of approximately 1,200 Israelis. However, international pressure for leniency shaped the Gaza barrier's design, leaving it more vulnerable.

Calls to improve the "optics" of Israeli policies also led to decisions that introduced critical security risks. In the months preceding October 2023, Israel increased the number of Gazans permitted to work in the country from 14,000 to 20,000. While the move aimed to alleviate Gaza's economic hardship, it also provided Hamas with insider access that enabled precision planning for the October 7 attack.

## The Events of October 7, 2023

At 6:30 a.m., Hamas launched over 5,000 rockets towards Israeli towns, forcing civilians to seek shelter. This barrage served as a prelude to a coordinated and multi-pronged assault. Reports indicate that Hamas breached the Gaza barrier at twenty-two locations, employing explosives, heavy machinery, and motorbikes to penetrate Israel's defences. Additionally, paragliders infiltrated kibbutzim, including Kfar Aza, where they executed a meticulously planned and devastating attack.

Insider knowledge—likely obtained from Gazan workers—enabled terrorists to target vulnerabilities. They seized armouries early, exploiting a government decree requiring weapons to be stored centrally. Defenceless civilians were ambushed, tortured, and murdered in atrocities that defy comprehension.

## A Moment for Accountability

Since October 7, 2023, the existential threat faced by Israel has become impossible to ignore. Under such circumstances, the condemnation of international voices—including the United Nations and activist organisations—becomes little more than white noise. As Israel rebuilds, it must reject external pressures that prioritise optics over security.

As the saying goes, "A bad headline is better than a good eulogy." Israel must prioritise its citizens' safety over appeasing critics. Francesca Albanese, the United Nations Special Rapporteur on the occupied Palestinian territories, epitomises toxic narratives by equating Israel's security measures with oppression while ignoring Hamas's actions. Such rhetoric fosters a worldview detached from reality and responsibility.

## Moving Forward

The October 7 attack underscores that security cannot be compromised for appeasement or political correctness. Israeli policies, often criticised as harsh, are life-saving measures for a nation under constant threat.

As Winston Churchill warned, "An appeaser is one who feeds a crocodile, hoping it will eat him last." The cost of appeasement has been measured in lives lost, communities devastated, and national security undermined.

The international community must confront its role in shaping the vulnerabilities exploited by Hamas and unequivocally support Israel's right to self-defence. Failing to do so risks allowing external actors who materially contributed to the massacre of innocent men, women, and children to escape accountability and culpability—an injustice that would compound the horrors of October 7 and set a dangerous precedent for the future.

6

# THE DECLINE OF GLOBAL INSTITUTIONS

## INTRODUCTION

History has a habit of presenting moments of reckoning—points at which individuals, institutions, and entire civilisations must choose between standing firm in the face of adversity or succumbing to complacency, corruption, and decay. The West is facing one such moment now, and the institutions we once relied upon to uphold justice and moral clarity are failing at an alarming rate.

For decades, international organisations such as the United Nations, Amnesty International, and the International Committee of the Red Cross (ICRC) were considered moral arbiters, guardians of human rights, and defenders of the oppressed. Yet, in recent years, these very institutions have become platforms for political manipulation, selective activism, and moral relativism. Nowhere is this hypocrisy more evident than in their treatment of Israel.

Israel's President Isaac Herzog captured this reality in his address to the United Nations on Holocaust Memorial Day, January 27, 2025. Echoing the words of his father, Chaim Herzog, who once tore apart the infamous "Zionism is Racism" resolution, he warned that the UN stands at a crossroads—between upholding the principles it was founded upon or descending further into irrelevance and ideological rot. His message was clear: Institutions that were once designed to serve justice must either reform or risk obsolescence.

This essay explores how global institutions have been compromised, how selective morality and institutional bias undermine their credibility, and what must be done to reclaim the integrity of the international order. As the West faces an existential test, we must decide—will we allow these once-noble institutions to continue their descent into hypocrisy, or will we demand accountability, reform, and a return to the fundamental values that once guided them?

The choice is ours.


## AT A CROSSROADS

*First published in The Australian Jewish News, April 9, 2025*

On Monday, January 27, 2025—Holocaust Memorial Day—Israel's President Isaac Herzog delivered a stark warning to the United Nations: The institution stands at a crossroads. Reflecting on his father Chaim Herzog's legacy, President Herzog invoked a profound familial and national history tied to the UN—a history marked by both triumphs and grave disappointments.

Chaim Herzog, as Israel's ambassador to the UN, became a defining figure in 1975 when he vehemently opposed the infamous "Zionism is Racism" resolution (UN General Assembly Resolution 3379). In a powerful act of defiance, Herzog tore the resolution apart in his speech, calling it a "lie" and a "desecration of Jewish history." The resolution was finally repealed in 1991, thanks to relentless efforts led by figures like US Ambassador Daniel Patrick Moynihan, who called the original resolution an "abomination." This long battle exemplifies both the UN's capacity for injustice and its potential for redemption.

President Herzog's speech underscored the dichotomy at the heart of the United Nations: It is both an arena for the pursuit of justice and a theatre for political manipulation. At its best, the UN represents hope for a more just world, a place where nations unite to prevent atrocities and promote peace. At its worst, it enables hypocrisy, allowing oppressive regimes to exploit its mechanisms while democracies face disproportionate scrutiny.

The UN's treatment of Israel has long embodied this paradox. While Israel has faced relentless condemnation in UN forums, the same institution has consistently failed to hold accountable some of the world's worst human rights violators. This moral inconsistency was central to President Herzog's address, challenging the global community to reconsider the UN's moral compass.

Yet, the UN is not alone—other transnational organisations and non-governmental bodies have also seen their credibility eroded by selective activism and institutional failure. These failures expose a broader crisis of legitimacy among institutions that once commanded trust but are now increasingly viewed as compromised and politically motivated.

## The Three Monkeys: Hear No Evil, See No Evil, Speak No Evil

The proverb of the Three Wise Monkeys encapsulates wilful ignorance—the refusal to acknowledge uncomfortable truths. This imagery is particularly apt in assessing the responses of major international organisations such as Amnesty International, the United Nations Human Rights Council (UNHRC), and the International Committee of the Red Cross (ICRC) to global crises, especially those involving Israel.

- **Hear No Evil – Amnesty International,** once a beacon of human rights advocacy, has increasingly turned a deaf ear to Israeli suffering while amplifying accusations against the Jewish state. Its selective outrage undermines its credibility, as it routinely ignores incitement, terrorism, and human rights abuses committed by groups openly dedicated to Israel's destruction.
- **See No Evil – The UNHRC,** with its numerous agencies and commissions, routinely ignores atrocities committed by autocratic regimes while relentlessly scrutinising Israel. Rather than being reformed by their inclusion, these regimes use their positions to deflect criticism and entrench their repression. Meanwhile, Israel—the Middle East's only democracy—faces obsessive and disproportionate scrutiny, remaining the only country permanently singled out for condemnation while genuine human rights violators go unchecked.
- **Speak No Evil – The ICRC,** mandated to uphold humanitarian principles, has demonstrated a troubling double standard regarding Israel. While it is quick to criticise Israel's defensive actions, it remains silent on violations committed by groups like Hamas. This bias is most glaring in the ICRC's failure to visit the hostages taken into Gaza on October 7, 2023. While it is accepted that Gaza remains a stronghold of violent extremists who revel in their war against the Jewish State, the ICRC's failure to even attempt a visit is a

dereliction of duty. Worse still, its continued silence is a moral abdication, calling into question its judgement, capacity, and commitment to its own humanitarian mandate.

This neglect represents a profound moral and operational failure. By not fulfilling its core mandate in these instances, the ICRC's impartiality and commitment to humanitarian principles are called into question. Organisations with noble missions risk enabling injustice through selective morality. To maintain credibility as impartial defenders of human rights, they must address all violations comprehensively, without bias.

## Manifest Failings

Amnesty International has also demonstrated clear bias. In February 2022, it released a report titled *Israel's Apartheid Against Palestinians: Cruel System of Domination and Crime Against Humanity*, accusing Israel of apartheid—a claim widely condemned as politically motivated. Israeli officials denounced the report as "false and biased," while the US State Department dismissed its conclusions as "absurd." The German Foreign Ministry rejected Amnesty's use of the term "apartheid," calling it unhelpful and inflammatory. Rather than applying consistent human rights standards, Amnesty International has increasingly peddled politically motivated narratives, undermining its credibility.

The ICRC, mandated to maintain neutrality in conflicts, has repeatedly been accused of bias regarding Israel and Hamas. During the 2023 Hamas-Israel war, the ICRC faced criticism for disproportionately highlighting the suffering of Gazan civilians while downplaying the plight of Israeli victims. It also failed to secure access to Israeli hostages held by Hamas, violating its own humanitarian mission. If an organisation designed to protect civilians in war cannot uphold its own basic principles, it loses the moral authority to operate as a neutral entity.

The UNHRC has a long history of disproportionately targeting Israel while downplaying or ignoring far more egregious human rights abuses. Qatar, despite its seat on the Council, has been condemned for its abuse of migrant workers and suppression of press freedom. Sudan, which held a UNHRC seat from 2021 to 2023 under military rule, continued to commit violent crackdowns on protests and war crimes in Darfur. Kenya, despite its election to the Council, has faced accusations of arbitrary arrests and enforced disappearances of government critics. Yet, Israel remains the only nation with a permanent agenda item—Agenda Item 7—ensuring that it is routinely condemned, regardless of actual events on the ground.

## Agenda Item 7: The UNHRC's Institutionalised Bias Against Israel

Agenda Item 7 is uniquely dedicated to scrutinising Israel at every UNHRC session, making it the only country in the world subject to permanent, institutionalised scrutiny. Established in 2006, it mandates that Israel be automatically debated under the heading, "Human rights situation in Palestine and other occupied Arab territories." This structure presupposes Israeli wrongdoing rather than assessing human rights violations objectively. Meanwhile, all other nations—regardless of their human rights records—are reviewed collectively under Agenda Item 4, shielding serial violators such as China, Iran, North Korea, and Venezuela from comparable scrutiny.

This systematic bias has led to an overwhelming number of resolutions condemning Israel, while ignoring severe abuses committed by Palestinian authorities, Hamas, and oppressive regimes worldwide. In October 2022, for example, the UNHRC rejected a proposal to debate China's human rights abuses in Xinjiang, despite credible reports of mass internment, forced labour, and repression of Uyghur Muslims. Yet, in the same session, Israel remained a primary target of condemnation. This blatant double standard enables dictatorships and theocratic regimes to escape accountability, while Israel—the Middle East's only democracy—is relentlessly vilified, regardless of the facts on the ground.

Many democratic nations and legal scholars have condemned Agenda Item 7 as discriminatory and politically motivated. In 2018, the United States and Australia called for its abolition, with US Ambassador Nikki Haley denouncing the UNHRC as a "cesspool of political bias." Canada, Germany, the UK, and the European Union have similarly criticised the Council's disproportionate focus on Israel, warning that it undermines the credibility of global human rights institutions. The UNHRC claims to defend universal human rights, yet its continued enforcement of Agenda Item 7 exposes a compromised institution, reinforcing diplomatic hostility towards Israel while allowing some of the world's worst human rights violators to act with impunity.

## Withhold Funds: Anticipate the Usual Tricks

Uncritical financial support has corrupted once-respected institutions, shielding them from scrutiny and accountability. Amnesty International, the ICRC, and other global bodies no longer uphold the standards that earned them trust—they have been infiltrated by activists who weaponise their influence for political agendas rather than their original mandates. Instead of remaining neutral arbiters of human rights, they have become vehicles for selective advocacy and agenda-driven litigation. If these institutions refuse to correct course, donor nations must reconsider funding, demand transparency, and enforce accountability.

The Austrian economist Joseph Schumpeter's concept of Creative Destruction—the dismantling of outdated institutions to make way for progress—is equally relevant to global governance. Stagnant, compromised institutions that resist reform must face obsolescence. The United Nations and its affiliates must recognise that their legitimacy depends not on their history or reputation but on their willingness to evolve— or be replaced. However, these organisations will not relinquish power without resistance.

Malicious compliance—adhering to reform demands while subverting their intent—will be their first line of defence. Expect superficial reforms, bureaucratic smokescreens, and symbolic gestures designed to placate donors while preserving the status quo. Institutions will manufacture crises, claiming that funding reductions will bring catastrophe—a classic Henny Penny "the sky is falling" routine.

Bloated, unaccountable organisations do not collapse when funding is cut—they adapt, streamline, or give way to better alternatives. As pressure for reform mounts, they may introduce committees, oversight panels, and token investigations, creating the illusion of accountability while entrenched ideological biases remain untouched. The strategy is simple: Delay, dilute, and deflect.

To break this cycle, real accountability must replace symbolic appeasement. Bureaucrats engaged in malicious compliance must be identified and removed, sending a clear message that obstruction will not be tolerated. Funding must be conditional on measurable benchmarks, external audits, and enforceable consequences for institutions that continue to prioritise politics over their mandates. The world must reject fear-mongering and scripted alarmism—international human rights depend not on preserving failed systems but on the willingness of these institutions to reform or be replaced.

## A Boost to Morale

The failures of these institutions are well-documented, backed by objective evidence of systemic dysfunction. However, this does not mean that everyone within them is complicit. Many dedicated individuals work tirelessly to uphold their missions, only to become disillusioned by a toxic culture where poor leadership enables bad actors to operate with impunity.

Nothing is more damaging to morale than witnessing corruption, bias, and incompetence go unchallenged. When accountability is absent, even the most committed professionals lose faith in the system they once believed in. Organisations do not fail because of the good people within them—they fail when those people are undermined, sidelined, or forced to conform to a broken culture.

The solution is clear: Keep the apple, remove the worms—but if the rot runs too deep, replace the apple altogether. Some institutions may be salvageable with strong leadership, decisive action, and the removal of entrenched corruption, allowing the remaining core to flourish once again. Others, however, may be beyond saving, their structures too compromised to function as intended. In such cases, clinging to a diseased apple only prolongs the inevitable decay. Where reform is impossible or resisted, new institutions must emerge—built on the same noble principles, but free from the rot that doomed their predecessors.

## At the Crossroads

President Herzog's warning is clear—the United Nations, along with Amnesty International and the ICRC, stand at a crossroads. Once trusted champions of human rights and global stability, these institutions have, in many cases, devolved into ideological echo chambers, prioritising political agendas over their founding principles.

The world is watching, and the stakes could not be higher. These institutions have a rare opportunity to reclaim their founding mission, but reform cannot be achieved through superficial adjustments or symbolic gestures. Accountability must come first. If reform fails, it will not merely disappoint member states and donors—it will betray the very ideals of justice, accountability, and global peace that these institutions were created to uphold.

The choice is clear: reform or irrelevance.

7

# LESSONS FROM HISTORY ON WHEN TO ACT

## INTRODUCTION

Decision-making in times of crisis is rarely straightforward. Leaders are often forced to choose between two difficult paths, knowing that neither will be free of consequences. The ability to navigate such dilemmas requires a guiding principle—one that prioritises long-term stability over short-term appeasement.

In politics, as in war, failing to act decisively can be just as dangerous as making the wrong choice. The current political climate in Australia, particularly regarding its shifting foreign policy and growing ideological divides, presents a stark example of leadership under pressure. Rising antisemitism, the erosion of bipartisan support for Israel, and the increasing influence of radical elements within mainstream parties demand a response that transcends political expediency.

This essay examines the historical shifts within Australian politics, particularly the trajectory of the Albanese government and the rising influence of minor parties. It argues that the erosion of the two-party system is leading to fragmented decision-making, with consequences that extend beyond domestic affairs and into Australia's position on the global stage.

At a time when the choices made by political leaders will determine the safety and cohesion of Australian society, this essay seeks to apply a guiding heuristic: When faced with difficult decisions, choose the path that, in time, will be regretted less.

## A GUIDING HEURISTIC

*First published in The Australian Jewish News, January 16, 2025*

## Introduction

"On the horns of a dilemma, do what in time you will regret less." This guiding principle has shaped my approach to life and leadership across two distinct careers. It speaks to making decisions when faced with two difficult options, where neither may initially seem ideal. As a soldier, this meant upholding standards and leading by example, often attracting criticism or unpopularity but knowing these actions could mean the difference between life and death in war. Now, as the CEO and Founder of The 2023 Foundation—a harm-minimisation charity dedicated to combatting antisemitism and fostering peaceful coexistence—it requires confronting structural failures in leadership. This, too, invites scrutiny and scorn, but at a time when antisemitic violence has reached unprecedented levels in Australia, silence is not an option.

Synagogues have been burnt, cars firebombed, and antisemitic graffiti like "Kill Israel" stains the walls of Australian cities. We appear to be living in an antebellum period—a moment of profound consequence before a storm. History offers no precedent where challenges of this magnitude have been resolved through inaction.

At the next federal election, Australians face a choice: a returned Albanese government (either as a majority or in alliance with the Teals and Greens) or a Dutton-led Coalition government. This article frames that decision, analyses the trajectory of the Albanese government, and advocates for the preservation of Australia's two-party system.

## A Personal Perspective

I grew up in a Hawke Labour household. The Australia of my youth was shaped by leaders like Bob Hawke, who brought people together and achieved significant reforms through bipartisanship. I see none of that legacy in the current Albanese government. Instead, the party has lurched to the left, no longer occupying the sensible centre of Australian politics.

I know Allegra Spender of Wentworth personally. I respect her as a person, a community leader, and a local member. She is someone who genuinely listens and engages thoughtfully. However, respect for an individual cannot overshadow the harsh realities we face as a nation. Synagogues are being burnt, cars firebombed, and antisemitic violence sweeps the nation. In this context, personal relationships and local representation are irrelevant compared to the broader structural challenges confronting our democracy.

## The Australian Labor Party (ALP)'s 1955 Moment

Labor faces an existential crisis reminiscent of its 1955 split, when a lurch to the left triggered the formation of the Democratic Labour Party. Then, it was communism that fractured the ALP. Today, it is the far left, whose influence risks alienating the party's traditional base.

This shift is most evident in foreign policy. The government's approach to Israel—evidenced by UN votes and statements—stands in stark contrast to Labor's historic commitment to Israel. The marginalisation of moderate voices has led to policy positions that undermine Australian values and compromise our national interests.

Australia's Prime Minister must recognise this inflection point as his Howard Moment. John Howard's decisive action following the Port Arthur massacre in 1996, where he introduced sweeping gun reforms despite strong resistance from elements of his political base, was one of the first bold moves in a career defined by prioritising the national interest over partisan concerns. This decision set a pattern of leadership that placed the greater good above political expediency, earning Howard respect across the political spectrum and cementing his legacy as a statesman.

For Prime Minister Albanese, the stakes are similarly high. He now faces a defining opportunity to demonstrate leadership that transcends party ideology and addresses the critical challenges of rising antisemitism and societal division. Bold, decisive action in this moment could shape his legacy and restore national confidence in his government while reaffirming Australia's commitment to unity and safety for all its citizens.

## The Rise of the Teals and Greens

The emergence of the Teals and the growing influence of the Greens are symptoms of a fractured political system. Teal Independents, while campaigning on local issues in traditionally Liberal electorates, frequently vote in alignment with Labor and the Greens on critical matters.

These voting patterns weaken the two-party system and contribute to a fragmented Parliament, where coalitions of disparate interests hinder effective governance.

The 2024 letter co-signed by several Teal MPs advocating for the restoration of funding to the United Nations Relief and Works Agency (UNRWA) highlights this issue. While the letter acknowledged allegations linking UNRWA employees to terrorism, it failed to address the organisation's structural flaws.

As Dr. Einat Wilf detailed in *The War of Return*, UNRWA perpetuates the Palestinian refugee narrative, obstructing peace efforts by refusing to address the root causes of the conflict. Advocacy for its funding without demanding reform reflects a troubling lack of understanding of the complexities on the ground.

## The Consequences of Fractured Politics

Australia's two-party system has historically provided stability, enabling governments to enact reforms and govern effectively. However, the rise of the Teals and Greens threatens this stability, creating a Parliament more akin to the Israeli Knesset, where coalitions of disparate interests struggle to achieve meaningful outcomes.

We must recognise the stakes: the firebombing of synagogues, rising antisemitism, and the erosion of trust in government institutions. These challenges demand clear and decisive leadership, not the fragmented alliances typified by minor parties.

## A Call to Action

Democracy, as Winston Churchill observed, is the worst form of government—except for all the others. The two-party system is not perfect, but it remains the best mechanism for delivering stability and accountability.

To Jewish Australians: Your vote matters. Stand tall and advocate for policies that ensure safety and cohesion for all.

To non-Jewish Australians: Recognise the stakes and stand against hate. Help create a Parliament that reflects our shared values, free from fragmentation and extremism.

As voters, we face a choice. Elections today are more consequential than at any other time in my lifetime. As Joseph de Maistre observed, "Every [democratic] nation gets the government it deserves." Let us start a conversation now to ensure that the government we elect in 2025 reflects the principles of justice, unity, and resilience that Australia so desperately needs.

# CONCLUSION TO SECTION IV

Western civilisation is at a breaking point.

It must decide: Will it stand for truth, democracy, and moral clarity, or will it surrender to ideological decay, appeasement, and cowardice?

This section has revealed the crumbling foundations of the modern West—the failures of leadership, the betrayal of values, and the consequences of appeasement.

The battle for Israel's survival is not separate from the battle for the survival of Western civilisation. They are one and the same.

The final section of this book will move from diagnosis to action—offering solutions, strategies, and a path forward for those willing to fight for civilisation.

# WINNING THE PEACE – THE PATH FORWARD FOR ISRAEL AND THE JEWISH PEOPLE

## INTRODUCTION TO SECTION V

Wars are not won solely on the battlefield. True victory is securing a just and lasting peace.

Israel has always been fighting for its survival, but it has never lost sight of its vision for peace. Unlike its enemies—who seek destruction, subjugation, and religious domination—Israel fights to live, to build, and to coexist.

The world often demands of Israel, "What is your endgame?" The truth is that Israel has always sought peace. But peace cannot come at the cost of security. The repeated failures of peace negotiations have not been due to Israeli unwillingness, but rather to the intransigence of those who reject Israel's very right to exist.

This final section outlines a path forward—not just for Israel but for all those who value truth, coexistence, and the defence of Western civilisation. It will explore what went wrong in past peace efforts, what must be done differently, and how Israel's success is intertwined with the future of the free world.

The stakes have never been higher. Will Israel merely survive, or will it finally win the peace?

# 1

# HOW SOCIAL MARXISM AND MEDIA BIAS SHAPE SOCIETY

## INTRODUCTION

We live in Orwellian times. Narratives are no longer shaped by facts but by ideological agendas. The reporting on Israel's military campaign in Gaza is not merely biased—it is a deliberate exercise in manipulation. The deceit, distortion, and outright lies that permeate media, academia, and political discourse are not isolated to Israel; they are symptomatic of a broader campaign to control public perception.

This essay builds on themes from "Gaslighting and Projection of Orwellian Proportion," examining how media bias, social Marxism, and political opportunism distort reality far beyond the Israeli-Palestinian conflict. It explores how the same forces driving misinformation about Israel are at play in other critical issues, from energy policy to foreign affairs. The manipulation does not stop at one topic—it is part of a systemic effort to shape how we think, who we trust, and what we believe.

By analysing historical parallels, the ideological capture of institutions, and the global consequences of accepting false narratives, this essay urges readers to see through the deception and reclaim their ability to think critically. Because if history has taught us anything, it is that the greatest danger lies not in what is being hidden, but in what we fail to question.

## WHILE MY GAZE WAS ELSEWHERE

*First published in The Australian Jewish News, December 30, 2024*

We live in Orwellian times. The deceitful and antisemitic reporting on the Israeli military campaign in Gaza is a glaring example of the gaslighting endemic in parts of the media, academia, and political discourse across the Western world. This article builds on themes from my earlier piece, "Gaslighting and Projection of Orwellian Proportion," to challenge whether this gaslighting stops at Israel and the Israel Defense Forces (IDF)—or if it is simply the most visible and egregious example of a broader manipulation.

### The Difference Between Persuasion and Manipulation

The distinction between persuasion and manipulation, in my judgement, lies in intent. Persuasion seeks to inform and inspire with philanthropic motives, aiming to foster understanding and thoughtful action. Manipulation, by contrast, operates with malign intent, seeking to deceive and control.

The reporting on Israel exemplifies manipulation, where distortion and bias have sown mistrust and misunderstanding. This raises broader concerns about the narratives promoted by certain media outlets, academics, and political actors—a pattern suggesting deeper systemic agendas. To better understand this phenomenon, it's worth looking back, as it becomes increasingly clear that this manipulation has been at play for some time.

## A Historical Lens: Begin and Reagan

Consider Menachem Begin and Ronald Reagan, two leaders whose legacies are now widely celebrated but who faced relentless vilification during their time in office.

Before his election as Israel's Prime Minister, Begin was labelled a threat to democracy. David Ben Gurion refused even to mention him by name, referring to him dismissively as "the man in the basement." Yet Begin achieved what many thought impossible: a peace treaty with Egypt, Israel's greatest adversary at the time.

Similarly, Reagan was dismissed as a "Hollywood actor turned politician," caricatured by critics as reckless and simplistic. Despite this, he ended the Cold War without firing a shot, revitalised the American economy, and restored confidence in democratic values.

The parallels with contemporary figures like Peter Dutton are striking. Leaders such as Australia's opposition leader are frequently castigated as "far right" by media, academia, and political opponents. But this raises an essential question: Is Dutton truly far right, or simply far right of those who now find themselves firmly entrenched on the far left?

## The Authors, Their Message, and Their Supporters

The same voices vilifying Israel and the IDF—sections of the Australian Broadcasting Corporation (ABC), certain academics, union agitators, and partisan journalists—are often those driving divisive narratives in other domains. Their coordination raises doubts about their trustworthiness and intent. If their approach to Israel is rooted in deception, can their messaging in other areas be trusted?

Take nuclear energy policy, for example—a subject outside my area of professional expertise, but one that deserves scrutiny. Across the globe, nuclear energy is increasingly seen as a critical component of a sustainable energy future. France generates over 70 percent of its electricity from nuclear power, making it a leader in low-carbon energy. Canada, too, has embraced nuclear energy as part of its strategy to reduce emissions, with prominent progressive figures like former Prime Minister Justin Trudeau advocating for its inclusion in achieving net-zero goals.

Even in Australia, former Prime Minister Bob Hawke—a revered Labor leader and iconic figure of progressivism—advocated for nuclear power as a forward-thinking solution to the nation's energy challenges. He argued that Australia's vast uranium reserves offered an unparalleled opportunity to reduce greenhouse gas emissions and ensure energy security while boosting economic growth.

Contrast this with the Albanese government. Prime Minister Anthony Albanese and Energy Minister Chris Bowen have consistently dismissed nuclear energy as a viable option, citing high costs and long lead times. Bowen recently called nuclear power "the most expensive form of energy," a claim that critics argue overlooks advancements in technology and the broader economic benefits of a diversified energy portfolio.

This shift also extends to foreign policy. For decades, there was bipartisan support for Israel's right to exist in peace and security, with successive Australian governments maintaining a steady alliance with Israel. Recent actions by the Albanese government, including changes in Australia's voting patterns at the United Nations, have been perceived by some as a departure from this bipartisan tradition. Critics argue that these moves align Australia with divisive UN resolutions that undermine Israel's legitimacy, reflecting a broader pivot from the consensus-driven foreign policy of earlier decades.

## Occam's Razor and Social Marxism

Occam's Razor, the principle that the simplest explanation is often the correct one, offers insight here. The simplest explanation for the consistent distortion in reporting, policymaking, and public discourse is that much of the left in politics, media, and academia has been overtaken by social Marxists.

Social Marxism applies Marxist principles to cultural and social structures rather than economic systems. It divides the world into oppressors and the oppressed, prioritising identity politics and victimhood narratives over truth and shared values. This framework not only explains the distorted reporting on Israel but also sheds light on the broader decay in public discourse across the Western world.

The connection between manipulation in media and social Marxism becomes clear when one examines how narratives are framed. The same individuals and institutions that distort facts about Israel often exhibit a broader agenda: discrediting traditional values, stifling evidence-based debate, and championing divisive ideologies.

## Lessons from Leadership

Ronald Reagan once warned, "Freedom is never more than one generation away from extinction." This cautionary statement resonates deeply in today's context, where ideological rigidity and social Marxism threaten to erode democratic resilience. Leadership in such times requires clarity, integrity, and the courage to stand against prevailing tides of manipulation and deceit.

Throughout my military career, I learnt the importance of valuing actions over rhetoric. Words can be empty vessels, but actions reveal true intent. This principle guided me as I observed sycophants who sought to curry favour through flattery while pursuing self-serving motives. The lesson was clear: Substance always outweighs superficiality.

This perspective informed my reaction to the recent US presidential election, when I observed a highly educated Australian Jew catastrophise over the election of the 47th President of the United States and its implications for reproductive rights. My own stance on this issue is pro-choice, yet I found the hyperventilation unwarranted, especially given the administration's stated policy of keeping abortions "safe, legal, and rare."

This episode revealed a deeper trend: a political platform so weak that the only strategy left was to vilify the alternative. Convincing the public that the alternative is worse is a hallmark of far-left politics, which relies on division and fear rather than constructive solutions.

## A Reflection

As I approach the conclusion of this article, I find it necessary to share my assessment: I, like many Australians, have at times been influenced by narratives shaped by social Marxists masquerading as educated and learned progressives. However, I have since begun to see through this manipulation. I encourage readers to take a moment of introspection—to reflect on some of the beliefs you may hold as incontrovertible truths. Who are the voices shaping these narratives, and what are their intentions? Because the same people who lecture us incessantly about genocide and apartheid are often the ones championing other causes, perceptions, and ideologies that I can no longer accept at face value.

Abraham Lincoln wisely noted, "You can fool all of the people some of the time, and some of the people all of the time, but you cannot fool all of the people all of the time." To this, I would add the enduring adage: "Fool me once, shame on you. Fool me twice, shame on me." Together, these sentiments remind us that discernment is not just a virtue but also a necessity, especially in these Orwellian times.

The reporting on Israel has taught me a vital lesson: to scrutinise, question, and seek truth—even when it challenges long-held beliefs. In these consequential times, clarity and integrity are not luxuries; they are imperatives. We have agency, and we must put a stop to this madness in 2025.

# 2

# THE COST OF HESITATION IN TIMES OF CRISIS

## INTRODUCTION

Hindsight is a powerful teacher. In moments of crisis, leaders are forced to make decisions that shape the course of history—some rise to the challenge, while others falter under the weight of hesitation or misplaced priorities. The aftermath of the October 9, 2023, events at the Sydney Opera House and the subsequent surge in antisemitic violence across Australia is a stark reminder of what happens when leadership fails to act with clarity and conviction.

This essay applies a counterfactual lens to these events, asking the following questions: What if decisive leadership had intervened at the right moments? What if those in power had responded with the urgency the situation demanded? Drawing from historical precedent and crisis leadership principles, it explores the path not taken—the actions that should have been taken to uphold public order, protect vulnerable communities, and restore faith in the rule of law.

The rise in antisemitic violence, government complacency, and media failures over the past twenty-three months should not just be cause for reflection—it must be a call for change. The lessons of inaction are now painfully clear. Will they be heeded?

## IF WE HAD OUR TIME AGAIN

*First published in The Australian Jewish News, January 8, 2025*

Several years ago, Viktor Frankl's *Man's Search for Meaning* resonated deeply with me. One quote stood out: "Live as if you were living for the second time and as though you had acted wrongly the first time." This profound statement invites us to approach life with the wisdom and reflection of hindsight, recognising past mistakes—or potential ones—and consciously choosing differently.

In these times of unprecedented antisemitic violence across Australia, fuelled by elements within the media, academia, and even fringe and major political parties, such reflection is urgent. Events over the past twenty-three months compel us to examine whether our actions—or inactions—have contributed to the current crisis and to consider what accountability truly looks like.

### Reflection Through the Australian Defence Force (ADF) Lens

The ADF employs the After-Action Review (AAR) as a cornerstone of continuous improvement. This process revisits events to identify what to "fix," "improve," and "sustain," with the aim of ensuring that we are better tomorrow than we were yesterday and are today. It's about learning from the mistakes of the past to guide decisions going forward.

A review's value may be heightened further by considering "the path not taken." By contrasting actual outcomes with hypothetical alternatives, we uncover valuable insights to guide future decisions. It is prudent to apply this reflective lens to events beginning on October 9, 2023, at the Sydney Opera House, and extending to today, January 2025.

## Recapitulation of Events

- **Hamas Attack on Israel (October 7, 2023):** Hamas launched a terrorist attack on Israel, killing more Jews in a single day than at any time since the Holocaust.

- **Sydney Opera House Illumination (October 9, 2023):** The Opera House was illuminated in blue and white to show solidarity with Israel. Initially, this decision inspired hope. Families planned to gather in solidarity, but NSW Police soon warned the Jewish community to "stay away" due to safety concerns. This effectively ceded public space to those who wished to intimidate and vilify.

- **Pro-Palestinian Protest (October 9, 2023):** Approximately 1,000 protesters marched from Town Hall to the Opera House, igniting flares and chanting slogans like "Allahu Akbar" and "Free Palestine." Some members of the Jewish community remain adamant that they heard the chant, "Gas the Jews."

- **Antisemitic Chants:** Forensic analysis later identified chants of "Where's the Jews" and offensive language like "F*** the Jews." For the Jewish community, this conclusion compounded their sense of betrayal.

- **Adass Israel Synagogue Arson Attack (December 6, 2024):** A Melbourne synagogue was firebombed, causing significant damage and traumatising the Jewish community.
- **Rising Antisemitic Incidents:** Reports of antisemitic incidents surged 316 percent between October 2023 and September 2024.
- **Physical Assaults and Vandalism:** Jewish cemeteries were desecrated, cars firebombed, and individuals wearing symbols of their faith attacked.
- **Online Hate Speech:** A marked increase in antisemitic hate speech created a pervasive atmosphere of hostility.

## Lived Experience

A non-Jewish friend in his seventies shared with me the profound distress of his Jewish neighbour in Woollahra. Seeking to offer support, he visited the octogenarian, only to find her too terrified to leave her upstairs room. "It happened just down the road," she said, her voice heavy with disbelief. "In a country and city we thought was safe."

Moved by her fear, my friend made a solemn vow: "If they come for you, it will be through me."

That conversation took place in October 2023. Today, I can only imagine how much worse her fears must be, compounded by the subsequent horror of two fire-bombings in Woollahra and the gutting of a Melbourne synagogue by arsonists.

How has it come to this in Australia in 2025?

## The Path Not Taken: A Case for Decisive Leadership

Accountability should be about meaningful outcomes, not hollow gestures. Decisive leadership in times of crisis can restore trust and reassure communities. Consider this alternative timeline:

- **10:00 p.m., October 9, 2023:** The premier's chief of staff summons the police minister for an 8:00 a.m. meeting.
- **7:00 a.m., October 10, 2023:** The prime minister and opposition leader jointly condemn the protest, standing on the Opera House steps to declare, "This must never happen again." (This idea, attributed to John Howard, reflects what he said he would have done with Kim Beazley in a similar situation.)
- **9:00 a.m., October 10, 2023:** The premier announces the police minister's resignation and appoints an interim replacement.
- **4:30 p.m., October 10, 2023:** An independent inquiry into police conduct is launched, led by a retired Federal Court judge and a former police commissioner, with a fourteen-day reporting deadline.
- **5:00 p.m., October 10, 2023:** The premier announces the police commissioner's resignation and appoints an interim replacement.

Decisive actions like these would have demonstrated resolve, boosted morale within the police force, and sent an unequivocal message: Law and order must prevail.

Such actions would not be without precedent. In 2014, Barry O'Farrell resigned as NSW premier after inadvertently misleading the Independent Commission Against Corruption (ICAC) over an undeclared gift—a bottle of wine. His resignation was not due to malfeasance but to uphold the principles of accountability and integrity. If accountability mattered then, why does it not matter now, in the face of such profound failings?

## Not a Criticism of Premier Minns

This is not a critique of Premier Chris Minns. On the contrary, Premier Minns has been a standout on both the state and national stage for his unflinching support of Australian values and his condemnation of bigotry and acts of domestic terrorism against Australia's Jewish minority. His leadership in these trying times has been commendable, setting a high standard for integrity and courage.

Prominent Jewish leaders have recognised and commended his principled stance. Rabbi Dr. Benjamin Elton, Chief Minister of The Great Synagogue in Sydney, has expressed appreciation for the Premier's commitment to protecting the Jewish community. Rabbi Levi Wolff, Senior Rabbi at Central Synagogue in Sydney, and Rabbi Mendel Kastel OAM, Chief Executive Officer of Jewish House, have similarly lauded Premier Minns for his proactive measures in ensuring the safety and well-being of Jewish Australians. David Ossip, President of the New South Wales Jewish Board of Deputies, has also been vocal in acknowledging the Premier's efforts to combat antisemitism.

However, this is most certainly a damning criticism of the Australian Labor Party and the broader left movement in Australia. The troubling alliance between leftist academics, unions, and some politicians has facilitated an environment where antisemitism can flourish unchecked. For example, certain NSW-based unions publicly endorsed pro-Palestinian rallies, even as these events became platforms for antisemitic rhetoric and violence. Left-leaning academics have published or endorsed statements justifying the actions of Hamas under the guise of "resistance." Meanwhile, some Labor politicians have hesitated to unequivocally condemn antisemitism, choosing instead to issue vague statements that fail to address the gravity of the issue. This silence and tacit endorsement amplify the challenges Premier Minns faces as a leader standing on principle in an otherwise indifferent or complicit environment.

But how much must be left on this one man's shoulders? Leadership at the top can only do so much without the collective support of institutions, including the media. Where were they in holding up the mirror to society during these dark times? Consider, for instance, the Australian Broadcasting Corporation (ABC), which has previously been critical of racism in other contexts. For example, the ABC has not hesitated to produce in-depth analyses, roundtable discussions, and investigative reports when discussing systemic racism affecting Indigenous Australians. Yet, in this crisis, their silence on the rise of antisemitism in Australia was deafening. Why, when antisemitic chants echoed at the Opera House and violence erupted across the country, did the media fail to address the issue with the same vigour?

## The Boiled Frog Syndrome

Australia risks becoming the proverbial frog in boiling water, failing to recognise the danger until it's too late. The escalation of antisemitic violence is a dire warning. Jewish Australians are asking: Where is the accountability? This question weighs heavily, not just on the Jewish community, but on all who value justice and safety.

This is not just a Jewish problem; it is a national one. Failing to act decisively now endangers the very fabric of Australia's values and democratic principles.

## Conclusion

As Viktor Frankl's words remind us, hindsight provides the wisdom to choose differently. Reflecting on the events of the past twenty-three months, it is evident that decisive action is not only warranted—it is imperative. Accountability at the highest levels must be pursued, and leadership grounded in resolve and a commitment to justice must guide Australia forward.

3

# A PATTERN OF PALESTINIAN REJECTION

## INTRODUCTION

Throughout modern history, Israel has repeatedly extended its hand in peace, only to have it slapped away. From the 1947 UN Partition Plan to the Oslo Accords and beyond, Palestinian leadership and its regional allies have consistently chosen rejection, violence, and intransigence over compromise and coexistence. This cycle of missed opportunities has not only prolonged the conflict but has deepened the suffering of generations on both sides.

This essay examines the pivotal moments when peace was within reach, only to be discarded in favour of war and ideological entrenchment. It explores the consequences of rejectionism, the role of international enablers, and the cultural and political forces that perpetuate conflict instead of resolution.

History has shown that peace is not won by slogans or diplomatic theatrics—it requires difficult choices, leadership, and a willingness to accept reality. Until the Palestinian leadership and its supporters abandon the delusion of Israel's destruction, the conflict will remain not one of two peoples, but of one people willing to coexist and another still unwilling to accept the other's right to exist.

# MISSED OPPORTUNITIES: WAR OVER COMPROMISE

*First published in The Australian Jewish News, January 7, 2025*

In 1948, the United Nations made a momentous decision to establish a Jewish state and an Arab state in the land of British Mandate Palestine. This historic resolution offered a foundation for two nations to coexist peacefully. However, the path since has been marked by a series of missed opportunities, lost lives, and entrenched divisions.

The State of Israel was born on May 14, 1948, amidst fierce opposition from neighbouring Arab states. While Israel's leaders accepted the UN Partition Plan, the Arab leadership rejected it, choosing war over compromise. As Golda Meir, one of Israel's founding leaders, famously observed, "We can forgive them for killing our children. We cannot forgive them for forcing us to kill their children. Peace will come when the Arabs love their children more than they hate us." This stark statement encapsulates the persistent barriers to peace—a prioritisation of conflict over the wellbeing of future generations.

## A History of Missed Opportunities

From the outset, opportunities for peace were repeatedly squandered. Abba Eban, the eloquent Israeli diplomat, once remarked that "the Arabs never miss an opportunity to miss an opportunity." The 1948 rejection of the Partition Plan was the first in a long list of such moments.

In 1967, following the Six-Day War, Israel offered to return captured territories in exchange for peace. The Arab League responded with the Khartoum Resolution: "No peace with Israel, no recognition of Israel, no negotiations with Israel." Again, the prospect of peaceful coexistence was set aside for intransigence.

The Oslo Accords in the 1990s brought a glimmer of hope. Israeli Prime Minister Yitzhak Rabin and Palestinian leader Yasser Arafat shook hands on the White House lawn under the auspices of US President Bill Clinton. Clinton, reflecting on these negotiations, later remarked, "The Palestinians have been given numerous opportunities to establish a state, and they have blown every one of them." Despite these efforts, the promise of Oslo unravelled amid mutual distrust, violence, and the rise of Hamas as a dominant force.

## Incentivising Bad Behaviour

The term "the occupation" has become a catch-all phrase with meanings that differ depending on who is speaking. For some, particularly those with genocidal intent, it refers to the very existence of Israel. For others, it relates to the divisions of the West Bank into Areas A, B, and C. However, the continued presence of the Israel Defense Forces (IDF) in these territories is, in my view, unavoidable until a Palestinian leader emerges who is willing to bury the hatchet and live peacefully with their Israeli neighbour behind internationally recognised borders.

Efforts by the United Nations and some antipodean nation-states are counterproductive, as they perpetuate the illusion that Palestinian intransigence will eventually yield results. Instead of encouraging compromise, these actions prolong the suffering of Palestinians who simply wish to raise their families free from politics and intrigue.

A line from *Hamilton: An American Musical* resonates here: "No one really knows how the parties get to yes. The art of the compromise—hold your nose and close your eyes." Genuine compromise requires difficult decisions, and the lack of Palestinian willingness to engage in such processes has been a consistent obstacle to peace.

## Palestinian Media and the Culture of Hatred

To understand why peace remains elusive, one must examine the pervasive narratives within Palestinian society. Groups like Palestinian Media Watch, led by Itamar Marcus, have meticulously documented how the Palestinian Authority (PA) fosters a culture of hatred through media, education, and public discourse.

Palestinian textbooks often glorify martyrdom and demonise Israel, while official media platforms broadcast incitement against Jews and Israelis. Facilities run by the United Nations Relief and Works Agency (UNRWA) have also been implicated in the radicalisation of Palestinian youth. For example, curricula in UNRWA schools glorify violence and perpetuate anti-Israel propaganda. A report by Palestinian Media Watch highlighted one instance where a UNRWA school celebrated a student essay describing the desire to "become a martyr."

These activities, funded in part by international taxpayers—including Australians—raise serious questions about accountability. When children are taught to view their neighbours as enemies and to aspire to violence, the foundations for peace are eroded before they can even be built.

## Corruption and Mismanagement

The leadership of Palestinian factions has further undermined progress. Reports have highlighted rampant corruption within both the PA (Fatah) and Hamas. High-ranking officials live in luxury while ordinary Palestinians face poverty and hardship. For example, Mahmoud Abbas, the President of the PA, has been criticised for amassing significant wealth, with some estimates suggesting a net worth of over $100 million. Similarly, Hamas leaders have enriched themselves while using international aid to build an extensive network of terror tunnels and armaments, rather than schools, hospitals, or infrastructure to benefit civilians.

Instead of transforming Gaza into a thriving society akin to Singapore, Hamas has turned it into a fortified enclave of despair—effectively a "fortress of conflict"—perpetuating war and stifling opportunities for peace.

## Changing Perspectives in Israel

The optimism that characterised the Oslo years has given way to a hardened realism among many Israelis. The two-state solution, once a widely supported goal, is now viewed by many as a dangerous fantasy.

The Second Intifada, which erupted in 2000, was a turning point. Suicide bombings and other acts of terrorism shook Israeli society to its core. The violence reinforced a sentiment that concessions are met not with peace but with greater hostility.

As of today, polls show a decline in Israeli support for the two-state solution. The notion of withdrawing from territories that could become staging grounds for further violence is, for many, untenable. Security concerns have eclipsed aspirations for a negotiated peace.

## Comparing Post-War Investments

The disparity in international aid allocation is striking. Between 1945 and 1952, the US invested approximately $2.3 billion (equivalent to $18 billion today) in rebuilding Japan. This investment transformed Japan into a prosperous democracy. In contrast, since 1948, Palestinians have received over $30 billion in aid—yet much of this has been mismanaged or diverted, failing to yield comparable societal progress.

Western nations must ask hard questions: Are we throwing good money after bad? Continued funding to the PA should be contingent on public affirmation of Israel's right to exist and demonstrable actions to normalise peace behind internationally recognised borders.

## Conclusion

As Israel celebrates its seventy-sixth anniversary—in a land where Jews have had a continuous presence for approximately 3,000 years, dating back to the time of King David and the establishment of Jerusalem as the capital of the ancient Kingdom of Israel around 1000 BCE—its achievements stand as a testament to resilience and determination. Yet, the shadow of unfulfilled peace continues to loom. The lessons of the past must serve as a guide for the future—a future where missed opportunities no longer define the narrative.

It is my assessment that if a viable peace partner were to emerge, there would be an overwhelming majority of Israelis who would support a genuine and durable peace plan. However, the realities on the ground demand an unavoidable truth: an IDF presence, with the backing of Abraham Accords partners, will likely remain necessary for the foreseeable future. This presence is essential to support deradicalisation efforts, counter-insurgency operations, and the stabilisation of the region.

The experience of UNRWA has demonstrated with stark clarity that such roles cannot be outsourced. International frameworks that perpetuate dependency and incitement must give way to structures that promote accountability, reconciliation, and peace. Australia, like other nations, must recognise that the vehicle for achieving these outcomes is not the United Nations—an institution compromised by antisemites and ideological zealots. Instead, the focus should be on supporting Israel, a democratic nation and the only country in the region where Jews, Muslims, Druze, and Christians live together in peace and dignity.

# 4

# INTIFADA: A WAR OF PROPAGANDA AND VIOLENCE

## INTRODUCTION

Western discourse on the Israeli-Palestinian conflict is often driven by myths, misinformation, and a selective reading of history. Nowhere is this more evident than in the modern embrace of the term "intifada," a word that has become a rallying cry on university campuses, in protest movements, and across social media. To the uninformed, it suggests resistance, justice, or liberation. But its historical reality is far darker: a campaign of orchestrated violence designed to destabilise Israel, terrorise its civilians, and perpetuate a state of conflict rather than peace.

The call for intifada—whether in the streets of Ramallah or on the steps of Western institutions—must be understood for what it truly is: a rejection of coexistence and a direct endorsement of violence against Israel and its people. The world has seen this unfold before. The First and Second Intifadas were not organic uprisings of an oppressed people but deliberate, well-funded campaigns driven by corrupt leadership, Islamist ideology, and the perverse incentives of international politics.

As a military officer seconded to a United Nations peace-keeping mission in Israel, I witnessed firsthand the realities that are often ignored in the West. The glorification of martyrdom, the systemic indoctrination of Palestinian youth, and the entrenched culture of victimhood—these are not ingredients for peace, but rather for perpetual war. The events of October 7, 2023, marked a new chapter in this conflict, proving that while the West continues to romanticise the idea of resistance, Israel is left to pay the price in blood.

This chapter will examine the history, ideology, and consequences of the intifadas—not as they are imagined by activists in New York or Sydney but as they truly exist: movements sustained by hate, corruption, and a deep-seated refusal to accept Israel's existence. To misunderstand intifada is to misunderstand the very nature of the Israeli-Palestinian conflict. And in a world increasingly defined by the war on truth, such misunderstandings come at a catastrophic cost.

## INTIFADA: MYTHS, REALITIES, AND CONSEQUENCES

*First published in The Australian Jewish News, March 11, 2025*

## Introduction

In recent times, Western university campuses have witnessed a surge in pro-Palestinian protests, with students and faculty chanting slogans such as "From the river to the sea, Palestine will be free" and calling for "intifada." While some may interpret intifada as a call for resistance—and to others, it might sound like an exotic new kale salad—its historical reality is far more complex and troubling.

This article sheds light on the intifadas and their historical causes, significance, and devastating consequences. By delving into the ideological foundations that fuel these uprisings—including Islamic teachings and political and economic motivations—we aim to expose the realities that many in the West fail to grasp. Understanding the past is crucial for interpreting present-day calls for intifada and assessing their potential repercussions.

## What Is an Intifada?

The word "intifada" originates from Arabic, meaning "shaking off" or "uprising." In an Islamic and geopolitical context, it has been used to denote violent resistance movements, particularly against Israel. The term has deep ideological roots in Islamic teachings and is linked to broader concepts such as jihad and resistance against perceived oppression.

## The Heart of the Conflict

At its core, the Israeli-Palestinian conflict is about Israel's right to exist as the Jewish state. Israel fights to live in peace behind internationally recognised borders, while Palestinian Arab factions—supported by regional backers—struggle to ensure that there is no Jewish state at all.

This reality is best captured by the well-known observation often attributed to Israeli diplomat and statesman Abba Eban: "If the Arabs laid down their weapons, there would be peace tomorrow. If Israel laid down its weapons, there would be no Israel."

This sentiment reflects the existential stakes of the conflict—where Israel seeks security and recognition, while its adversaries, from Hamas to the Palestinian Authority (PA), continue to advocate for its destruction rather than coexistence.

## Dar al-Harb and Dar al-Islam

To fully understand the concept of intifada, one must examine the Islamic doctrine of *Dar al-Harb* (House of War) and *Dar al-Islam* (House of Islam). In this worldview, the world is divided into two spheres: lands governed by Islamic law (Dar al-Islam) and those that are not, which are considered to be in a state of conflict until they are brought under Islamic rule (Dar al-Harb).

Radical Islamist groups use this framework to justify perpetual conflict, particularly against Israel, which they view as an illegitimate entity occupying Muslim land. The rhetoric of intifada stems from this ideology, portraying Israel as an occupier that must be removed by force.

## The First Intifada (1987—1993): A Grassroots Uprising

The First Intifada erupted in December 1987, sparked by a traffic accident in the Gaza Strip, in which an Israeli military vehicle collided with a Palestinian car, killing four passengers. While the incident itself was unintentional, it ignited long-standing Palestinian grievances, triggering a widespread uprising.

What began as spontaneous unrest in Gaza quickly spread to the West Bank and East Jerusalem. Unlike previous conflicts, largely orchestrated by established political factions, the First Intifada was driven by grassroots activism. Palestinians engaged in widespread protests, economic boycotts, tax resistance, and violent attacks against Israeli security forces and civilians. In response, Israel imposed curfews, carried out mass arrests, and deployed the military to flashpoint areas. Israeli soldiers faced violent riots, with Molotov cocktails, stones, and other projectiles hurled at them. The Israel Defense Forces (IDF)'s use of rubber bullets, tear gas, and detention policies drew international scrutiny.

Western media broadcast powerful images of young Palestinians confronting Israeli troops, shaping global perceptions. While many saw the uprising as an expression of Palestinian aspirations for self-determination, others noted the role of regional actors in sustaining hostilities. After nearly six years of unrest, the First Intifada lost momentum, leading to renewed diplomatic efforts. The 1991 Madrid Conference and the 1993 Oslo Accords marked significant steps towards peace, culminating in mutual recognition between Israel and the Palestine Liberation Organization (PLO).

The Oslo Accords established the PA and granted it limited self-rule in parts of the West Bank and Gaza Strip. However, hopes for lasting peace were soon undermined by continued violence, including Hamas-led suicide bombings in Israeli cities and Israeli countermeasures. The 1995 assassination of Israeli Prime Minister Yitzhak Rabin further destabilised the peace process, while subsequent negotiations—such as the 1998 Wye River Memorandum—attempted but failed to resolve key disputes.

## The 2000 Camp David Offer

Tensions continued to rise as Palestinian frustration over Israeli settlement expansion and Israeli security concerns over persistent terrorism created a volatile situation. By the time Israeli Prime Minister Ehud Barak and Palestinian leader Yasser Arafat met at Camp David in July 2000, under the mediation of US President Bill Clinton, the peace process was already fragile.

The summit represented the most comprehensive attempt to resolve the conflict up to that point, yet it ultimately failed, setting the stage for the far more violent Second Intifada. The terms presented to Arafat by Israeli Prime Minister Ehud Barak, under US mediation, included the following:

1. **West Bank**: Palestinian control over 91–94 percent, with 1–3 percent land swaps from pre-1967 Israeli territory to compensate for settlement blocs
2. **Gaza Strip**: Full 100 percent Palestinian sovereignty
3. **East Jerusalem**: Palestinian sovereignty over Arab neighbourhoods, with some form of shared control over the Temple Mount/Haram al-Sharif
4. **Refugees**: No full "Right of Return," but provisions for compensation, resettlement in Palestine, and a limited symbolic return
5. **Security Arrangements**: Israel to retain a temporary strategic military presence in key areas

Despite these terms, the Palestinian leadership rejected the proposal and failed to provide any counteroffer. The failure of Camp David was followed by the outbreak of the Second Intifada, further deepening the conflict.

## The Second Intifada (2000—2005): A Devastating Escalation

The Second Intifada, or *Al-Aqsa Intifada*, erupted in September 2000. While Ariel Sharon's visit to the Temple Mount is often cited as the immediate trigger, this is disingenuous as the roots of the uprising lay in corruption, manipulation, intolerance, and an unwillingness to compromise.

In the years leading up to the Second Intifada, diplomatic efforts attempted to bring about a lasting peace. The 1993 Oslo Accords had established the PA as a governing entity, and by the late 1990s, there was cautious optimism that a two-state solution could be realised. Israeli Prime Minister Ehud Barak offered substantial concessions, including Palestinian sovereignty over much of the West Bank and Gaza, shared administration of Jerusalem, and even discussions on refugee issues. Yasser Arafat, however, rejected the offer outright—without proposing a counteroffer. His refusal marked a turning point, confirming to many that the Palestinian leadership was more interested in perpetuating conflict than in achieving statehood. Many Palestinians saw the summit's failure as proof that diplomacy could not deliver their aspirations.

What began as protests quickly escalated into an armed insurgency. Palestinian militants launched an unprecedented campaign of violence, characterised by suicide bombings, sniper attacks, and large-scale terrorist operations targeting Israeli civilians. Hamas, Islamic Jihad, and elements within the PA orchestrated attacks in cafes, buses, and shopping centres, murdering men, women, and children in a deliberate campaign of terror. The Palestinian leadership, rather than condemning the violence, encouraged and rewarded it, with the PA paying stipends to the families of "martyrs."

In response, Israel launched military operations to neutralise terrorist networks. The IDF carried out incursions into Palestinian-controlled areas, targeted senior militants for elimination, and constructed the West Bank security barrier—a defensive measure that significantly reduced terrorist attacks in subsequent years.

The Second Intifada resulted in over 1,000 Israeli deaths and thousands of Palestinian casualties. It shattered any remaining trust between the two sides, leading to the near-total collapse of the peace process. The international community, misled by a narrative of Palestinian victimhood, responded with misplaced sympathy—sending vast amounts of financial aid to the Palestinian authorities, much of which was siphoned off by corrupt officials. Rather than being invested in infrastructure or economic development, these funds were funnelled into the personal accounts of Palestinian leaders, further entrenching their incentive to sustain the conflict rather than resolve it.

## President Clinton's Reflections on the Collapse of Camp David

At the *New York Times* DealBook Summit in December 2024, former US President Bill Clinton reflected on the 2000 Camp David Summit, a pivotal moment in the Israeli-Palestinian peace process. He expressed frustration over the collapse of negotiations, attributing the failure to Yasser Arafat and his refusal to accept a deal that would have established a Palestinian state.

Clinton outlined the far-reaching concessions offered during the talks, including the establishment of a Palestinian capital in East Jerusalem and Israel's withdrawal from pre-1967 territory with a land swap to compensate for settlement blocs. Israel had also proposed full Palestinian sovereignty over Gaza and a limited but symbolic refugee resettlement arrangement. Despite these terms, Arafat rejected the offer without proposing an alternative, a decision widely seen as a major setback for peace.

Reflecting on the reactions of younger generations, Clinton observed that many young Americans are surprised to learn that Arafat rejected the opportunity for a Palestinian state under favourable conditions. He emphasised that this historical fact often catches them off guard, as they are more familiar with the broader narrative of the conflict than its pivotal moments. His remarks highlighted the crucial role of education in helping younger generations grasp the complexities and missed opportunities that have shaped the present reality.

## The Shadow of a Third Intifada (2020—Present)

Between July 2019 and September 2021, I lived in Jerusalem while seconded to the United Nations as a senior officer within an unarmed military peacekeeping mission. During this time, I witnessed a rising wave of violence that often felt like the early stages of a Third Intifada.

Jerusalem experienced a series of violent incidents, heightening tensions in the region. On February 21, 2020, a Palestinian woman attempted to stab passersby at the Armon Hanatziv promenade. Around the same period, a vehicle hit-and-run attack near Jerusalem's First Station, a popular entertainment district, reinforced the sense of growing instability. These incidents were not isolated; rather, they were part of a broader escalation of violence across Judea, Samaria, and the Gaza Strip.

My role provided me with frequent opportunities to engage in conversations with highly educated Palestinians—both Christian and Muslim Arab professionals—who lived in the West Bank and were bussed into Government House in East Jerusalem, Israel (or, as the UN often referred to it, "no-man's land") for their duties. A recurring theme in these discussions stood out to me: a deepening disillusionment with the Palestinian leadership, particularly Mahmoud Abbas.

Many educated Palestinians, including Arab Christians, acknowledged the corruption of their own leaders but saw no alternative to the entrenched status quo. What horrified and shocked me was that they believed the answer was to elect Hamas. Even more striking was how many of these individuals—particularly UN employees—defined "the occupation" not as Israel's presence in the West Bank, but as Israel's very existence. This gave me a stark insight into how radical the region was and how unwilling to compromise the Palestinians were.

Mahmoud Abbas has been a catastrophic failure, yet the alternative—Hamas—is even worse. His prolonged grip on power, now in its nineteenth year of what was meant to be a four-year term, highlights both the dysfunction of Palestinian governance and the grim reality that, until President Trump's 2025 White House announcement on resettling Palestinians in neighbouring countries, the only viable political alternative was a terrorist organisation that thrives on perpetual conflict.

One of the most significant miscalculations of the Palestinian leadership was Mahmoud Abbas's outright refusal to engage with the Trump administration's *Peace to Prosperity* initiative between 2018 and 2020. While the plan was imperfect, it presented another historic opportunity to redefine Palestinian self-governance through economic incentives and infrastructure investment. Yet, true to form, Abbas rejected it outright, refusing even to negotiate. His actions were part of a long pattern of Palestinian leaders sabotaging their own opportunities—embodying Abba Eban's famous observation: *"The Arabs never miss an opportunity to miss an opportunity."*

At the time, I had only a partial grasp of the deeper forces at play—the staggering influx of Western aid flowing into Palestinian coffers, the systemic corruption that diverted these funds from the people to the ruling elite, and the Palestinian leadership's perverse incentive to perpetuate conflict rather than pursue peace.

After the horrors of October 7, 2023, this reality is now undeniable.

## Follow the Money: Corruption in Palestinian Leadership

Amid the ongoing Israeli-Palestinian conflict, rampant financial corruption among Palestinian leaders has severely eroded the credibility of their governance. While ordinary Palestinians endure economic hardship, reports have exposed officials siphoning off aid funds meant for infrastructure and social services, instead amassing personal fortunes at the expense of the very people they claim to represent.

Yasser Arafat, the late leader of the PLO and the PA, was long suspected of diverting public funds for personal use. In 2003, the International Monetary Fund (IMF) reported that Arafat had transferred approximately $900 million in public funds to accounts under his direct control. These funds, which should have been allocated to improving the lives of Palestinians, instead disappeared into a web of financial secrecy. Following Arafat's death in 2004, his widow, Suha Arafat, reportedly received €1 million per month from the PA. While ordinary Palestinians struggled with economic instability, she resided in luxurious accommodations in France and Tunisia, far removed from the conditions endured by those still living under PA rule.

Mahmoud Abbas, who succeeded Arafat as President of the PA, has also faced serious allegations of financial misconduct. Despite drawing a modest official salary, his personal net worth is estimated to be around $100 million. His sons, Yasser and Tareq Abbas, have amassed wealth through business dealings that directly benefit from their father's political influence. Their ventures have included monopolies on American-made cigarettes sold in Palestinian territories, lucrative USAID-funded projects, and exclusive public works contracts. The Abbas family's accumulation of wealth has further entrenched public perceptions of widespread corruption within the Palestinian political establishment.

Hamas, the Islamist group that has ruled Gaza since 2007, has also fostered a culture of corruption while maintaining the facade of a resistance movement. Khaled Mashal, a former chairman of Hamas's Political Bureau, has resided in Qatar for years and is estimated to have amassed a personal fortune of approximately $2.6 billion. Mousa Abu Marzouk, another senior Hamas leader, has been implicated in financial dealings that have enriched him significantly, with his net worth estimated at $2.3 billion. While Hamas claims to fight for the Palestinian cause, its leaders enjoy lavish lifestyles abroad, while the people of Gaza suffer from economic deprivation, lack of basic infrastructure, and perpetual cycles of violence.

This entrenched corruption fuels public disillusionment and perpetuates the conflict. Palestinian leaders, instead of working towards a peaceful and prosperous future for their people, have prioritised personal gain. The billions in international aid that pour into Palestinian territories have not translated into economic growth or improved living conditions. Instead, they have reinforced the power of a corrupt elite who have no incentive to end the conflict—because war and victimhood ensure a continued flow of funds.

## A Cautionary Conclusion

*"Be careful what you wish for; you may receive it."*

The intifada has become a *cause célèbre* for Western university students, many of whom passionately denounce perceived oppression without a genuine understanding of the conflict's historical and ideological roots. Their inability to distinguish right from wrong, compounded by a glaring lack of moral clarity, is deeply troubling. What they fail to grasp is that the movements they champion are not driven by freedom or justice but are instead orchestrated by corrupt, self-serving leaders who exploit Palestinian suffering for personal and political gain.

Free speech is fundamental to any free society, but rights should never be divorced from responsibilities. In the West, those who support the intifada generally fall into three categories: Islamists and their sympathisers, who openly or covertly endorse jihadist violence; hard-left zealots and ideologues, who latch onto radical causes as a means of dismantling Western institutions; and useful idiots swept up in the rhetoric. The first group sees the conflict as part of a broader religious and geopolitical struggle, while the second exploits it as yet another front in their war against capitalism, democracy, and Western values. The third, blissfully unaware of the forces they are aligning with, mindlessly parrots slogans and embraces the cause as a fashionable form of activism, oblivious to the dangerous ideologies they are helping to legitimise and spread.

In confronting these threats, the response must be firm and unequivocal. Those who openly support terrorist organisations or incite violence should face serious consequences, including deportation, incarceration, and permanent records that impact future employment prospects. Universities and workplaces must take a stand against ideological extremism masquerading as activism, refusing to provide a platform for those who champion violence under the guise of social justice. A society that tolerates calls for intifada on its streets or campuses without consequence will inevitably find itself fighting the very forces it failed to confront—only at far greater cost.

# 5

# DEFYING DARKNESS AND DEFENDING TRUTH

## INTRODUCTION

As history has shown, moments of profound crisis demand more than just reflection—they require conviction, action, and unwavering moral clarity. The events of recent years, culminating in the October 7 attacks and the wave of antisemitism that followed, have exposed the stark reality that our time is not one of neutrality, but one of choice. Those who value freedom, truth, and Western civilisation must decide whether they will stand up or shrink into silence.

This essay, structured around nine fundamental truths, serves as both a warning and a call to action. It lays out the defining challenges of our era—from the resurgence of antisemitism to the collapse of institutional integrity—and offers guiding principles for those who refuse to be bystanders. Each point underscores the urgency of this moment and the role we all must play in ensuring that the values we hold dear are not extinguished.

Now is not the time for complacency. Now is the time to stand, to speak, and to act.

## NINE POINTS

*First published in The Australian Jewish News, January 24, 2025*

On the evening of December 22, 2024, the Mizrachi Synagogue in North Bondi hosted a landmark event titled "The Empowered Jew." Founded by Chavi Israel, The Empowered Jew is a not-for-profit organisation dedicated to equipping members of the Jewish community with the knowledge, skills, and confidence to advocate effectively for their heritage and Israel. Chavi, a Jewish studies educator at Moriah College, has channelled her passion for Jewish empowerment into creating a platform that fosters education and engagement.

The evening was graced by four speakers, all non-Jewish, each bringing a unique perspective to the challenges and opportunities facing the Jewish people today. Shoshana Eisner, an esteemed community leader, served as master of ceremonies, guiding the evening with poise and purpose. It was an honour to be invited to participate in this event and deliver a speech titled "Nine Points":

Australians, esteemed members of the Sydney Jewish community, ladies and gentlemen, good evening. I have nine points.

**One:** There is no precedent in human history where the challenges of the 1930s, or what we are witnessing in Australia today, miraculously fix themselves. Quite the opposite. Resolution demands leadership and resolve. For those who read *The Australian Jewish News* or have visited my website, you already know my thinking here. Things will worsen further before they begin to improve. But improve they will—through our actions and on our shoulders.

**Two:** The people who threaten you and your children also threaten me and mine. The world in which we live is known to the family and loved ones of poor Lee Rigby—and by those Israeli soccer fans set upon in Amsterdam in a pogrom in November 2024. We must not fail to recognise the zeitgeist, the spirit of our time.

**Three**: We will win in the end. If we are not winning, it is not the end. Remain of good spirit and continue to burden-share.

**Four**: The antisemitism sweeping through Australia and the Western world is not just a Jewish problem—it is a civilisational problem. It is an Australian problem. It threatens our shared values and our way of life.

**Five**: We live in Orwellian times. Where Hamas propaganda is parroted uncritically, and where two plus two is made to equal five. Please read or re-read Orwell's *1984* before Australia Day, 2025. I quote here from my dear friend Laura Taitz: "reading George Orwell's 1984 at school in the '80s was uneasy for me. Part of me desperately wanted to believe that no way something like that could ever happen, and part of me knew absolutely that it could definitely happen. "1984" should have been titled "2024." We are living in the time of 'gaslighting and projection of Orwellian proportion'."

**Six**: Institutions across the Western world are buckling under the weight of dishonesty and ideological extremism. Yet truth still matters. Honesty must be our guiding principle if we are to navigate this storm.

**Seven**: History reminds us that indifference is a luxury we cannot afford.

**Eight**: There are many examples from the past that frighten, but there are also those that inspire. As Golda Meir once said, "trust yourself. Create the kind of self that you will be happy to live with all your life."

**Nine**: The helper candle. I will not be a bystander as Israelis are gaslit and vilified. I will not remain silent as Jewish Australians are pilloried, intimidated, and subjected to violence and terrorism. I will not meekly acquiesce as the Judeo-Christian values of Australia, the land of my birth, are debased. As Ronald Reagan wisely remarked, "freedom is never more than one generation away from extinction. It must be fought for, protected, and handed on."

Across a thirty-year military career in the profession of arms, I have learnt that it is in adversity that the strength of our character is forged. It is during these times that we quickly identify those we can depend on and those we can trust. Jewish mysticism speaks of the existence of thirty-six hidden righteous individuals in every generation who sustain the world through their virtue.

This concept highlights the values of humility, hidden acts of kindness, and the profound impact of righteousness on the collective good. I'm on the lookout for those thirty-six. Once I find them, I will partner and collaborate with them. In the lead-up to Chanukah, my dear friend Yossi Eshed from the Zionist Council and Isra-Aid, passed me a beautiful message about the importance of lighting candles. When we light a candle, we all have "more light" and warmth. Help me spread the light and build warmth by amplifying my message and empowering me as an ambassador of light.

In conclusion, ladies and gentlemen, we each have a role to play. Great burdens are best carried forward into a better tomorrow on the shoulders of the many, the willing, and the able. With toil, conviction, and resolve, we will see better days. It is an honour to be here tonight, speaking at "The Empowered Jew." While I am not Jewish or Israeli, I may as well be. Because

I am with you in bad times and good—until we prevail. Thank you, my dear friends. Am Yisrael Chai!

The event concluded with a shared sense of purpose, inspired by the speakers' diverse yet complementary messages. "The Empowered Jew" exemplifies the strength and resilience of the Jewish community, united in its mission to confront challenges and empower future generations.

6

# THE RESPONSIBILITY TO STAND FIRM

## INTRODUCTION

Throughout history, light has been a symbol of hope, courage, and resilience in the face of oppression. Chanukah is not just a story of the past—it is a message for our time. The Maccabees' victory over tyranny reminds us that darkness is not defeated by fear, but by those willing to stand firm and push back.

On the evening of January 1, 2025, in the heart of Sydney, I had the honour of addressing a community gathered for the final night of Chanukah. The significance of this moment extended beyond the celebration of a festival—it was a rallying call in a time of rising antisemitism, societal division, and the erosion of values that once bound us together.

This essay captures that moment and the urgency behind it. We cannot afford complacency. The resurgence of antisemitism is not just an attack on Jewish communities—it is a test of the moral fabric of our society. History has shown that hatred left unchecked never remains contained; it spreads, consuming the weak and the silent.

Chanukah's lesson is clear: We must choose to be the light. Whether through words, actions, or unwavering support for those under attack, each of us has a role to play. The darkness we face today is great, but even the smallest flame can drive it back. The time to shine is now.

## IT'S TIME: FOR OUR LIGHT TO SHINE

*First published in The Australian Jewish News, January 26, 2025*

On the evening of January 1, 2025, under the soft glow of Hyde Park's evening lights, I had the honour of addressing members of the Sydney community during the final night of Chanukah at a public event. Hosted by Rabbi Danny Yaffe, Rebbetzin Sara-Tova Yaffe, and CBD Chabad, this event was a profound reminder of the resilience of the Jewish people and the enduring relevance of Chanukah's message for all Australians.

### The Significance of Chanukah

Chanukah, the Jewish "Festival of Lights," commemorates the rededication of the Second Temple in Jerusalem during the second century BCE. Against the odds, the Maccabees, a small band of Jewish fighters, triumphed over the Seleucid Empire, reclaiming their right to religious freedom. The miracle of the menorah, where a day's supply of oil burnt for eight days, symbolises the enduring power of faith and resilience.

For over two millennia, Chanukah has carried the timeless message that light can dispel even the deepest darkness. It reminds us that courage and unity are vital in overcoming adversity. For Australians, this message resonates strongly, urging us to combat hatred and division with hope and determination.

## Rally of Light — A Call to Action

The following is the full text of my speech, as delivered that night:

Good evening, my dear friends—esteemed members of the Sydney Jewish community—distinguished guests, ladies and gentlemen,

My name is Michael Scott. For thirty years, I served as a soldier in the Australian Army. Last year, I founded The 2023 Foundation, a nascent global harm-minimisation charity dedicated to combatting antisemitism and fostering peaceful coexistence. I am not Jewish, but in these troubled times, I may as well be, because I am with you.

It is such an honour to be here today. We have so much in common. Like you, I am a proud Australian. I am a patriot, a husband, and a father. Like you, I cherish the values that make our nation great: fairness, tolerance, and a commitment to a brighter future.

But tonight, I stand before you not just as a former soldier or the leader of a foundation—I stand here as an Australian, shoulder to shoulder with you, determined to dispel the darkness of hatred and division that threatens the values we hold dear.

Tonight, on this final evening of Chanukah, we gather under the banner of light—a light that has burnt in the Jewish soul for over 2,000 years and that now calls on all of us, regardless of our faith, to come together as Australians to stand against darkness.

**The Lessons of Chanukah:** Chanukah is a celebration of miracles, courage, and enduring faith. It reminds us of the triumph of light over darkness, of a small band of the faithful standing against a mighty force of oppression.

It teaches us that even when the odds seem insurmountable, the flicker of a single flame can ignite a blaze of hope.

But Chanukah is more than a commemoration of past miracles; it is a call to action. The menorah reminds us of our duty to spread light, one candle at a time, until the entire world is illuminated. Tonight, we kindle the final and brightest light of Chanukah—a symbol of hope, unity, and resilience.

Former Prime Minister John Howard once said, "The values we share as Australians—respect for each other and the celebration of difference—must never be taken for granted. They are the foundations of our strength." Chanukah challenges us to uphold these values, not just in words but in action.

**The Darkness We Face:** In recent years, we have witnessed a troubling resurgence of antisemitism—not just overseas, but here in Australia. This darkness manifests in vile words, insidious stereotypes, and even acts of violence. But antisemitism is not just a Jewish problem; it is a symptom of a deeper illness that threatens the fabric of our society.

Where there is hatred for one group, hatred for others soon follows. Racism, bigotry, and division are all intertwined. Combatting antisemitism, then, is not just a Jewish imperative—it is an Australian imperative.

Our country was born 124 years ago, on January 1, 1901, when six colonies united to form the Commonwealth of Australia through Federation. This historic day was not just about political unity; it was about forging a national identity rooted in shared values. Those values—fairness, inclusion, and a belief in the dignity of every individual—remain our greatest strength. Let us honour the spirit of Federation by defending those values against hatred and division.

As General Sir Peter Cosgrove so aptly put it, "A society is judged not by how it treats its strongest, but by how it supports its most vulnerable."

Let us take this lesson to heart and stand together against the forces that seek to divide us.

**It's Time to Shine Our Light:** Chanukah teaches us that a little light dispels much darkness. And while we may feel overwhelmed by the challenges before us, the lesson of the menorah is clear: Each of us has a light to share. Each of us can be a source of hope.

Tonight, as we gather in Hyde Park—where we have seen and heard darkness and ignorance so often this past year—let this moment stir and inspire us to action. Just as the Maccabees stood firm against oppression, so too must we stand against antisemitism, against division, and against hate. The Maccabees had agency; we do too!

This is not a task for one group or one community. It is a shared responsibility. Christians, Muslims, Jews, Hindus, Buddhists, atheists—all Australians must unite to defend our values of tolerance, respect, and justice. If values are not defended, they are not merely lost, but rather replaced by a void where division and oppression thrive. We live in Orwellian times; this is an Orwellian future we must recognise and resist with unwavering resolve.

**Practical Steps Forward:** To truly spread light, we must pair our words with deeds. As we celebrate Chanukah, let us also commit to four actions that dispel darkness:

- **One – Educate:** Teach all of Australia's children the dangers of hatred and the beauty of diversity.

- **Two – Advocate:** Speak up! Call out antisemitism and bigotry wherever we see it—in our workplaces, schools, and communities.
- **Three – Connect:** Build bridges with those who are different from us, fostering understanding and unity.
- **Four – Do Good:** Perform acts of kindness, however small, to make the world a brighter place. Empower and enable Ambassadors of Light and, in doing so, become one yourself.

As Julia Gillard once said, "When we treat each other with respect and fairness, we strengthen the fabric of our communities." Let us weave that fabric with threads of light and hope.

**A Personal Commitment:** When I founded The 2023 Foundation, it was out of a deep conviction that silence is not an option. My wife and I would not be bystanders. History shows us where the path of indifference leads. And as a soldier, I know this truth well: Evil thrives when good people do nothing.

To reiterate, I am with you—not just tonight, but every step of the way. In bad times and good, for as long as it may take. Until we prevail!

I know that Jewish Australians are among the finest Australians. This is a truth that must be demonstrated until the darkness is dispelled. I know that Australians look after their mates, particularly when their mates need them. In 2025, this should be both our guiding light and aiming mark—because what we saw in 2024 was not okay. It was not Australian.

**Chanukah's Eternal Message:** Tonight, as we light the final candle of the menorah, let it serve as a beacon—not just for the Jewish people, but for all Australians. Let it remind us of the power of resilience, the importance of hope, and the unbreakable strength of unity.

As the Rebbe once said, "A little light dispels a lot of darkness." My friends, it's time. It's time for our light to shine. May the light of Chanukah inspire us all to be better, to do better, and to build a brighter future for our nation and the world. Thank you. Am Yisrael Chai!

The convergence of the first day of Chanukah with Christmas Day is rare. These two significant holidays offer a unique opportunity for interfaith families and communities to celebrate shared values of light, hope, and resilience. It encourages mutual respect and understanding between Jewish and Christian traditions, fostering a sense of unity during the festive season.

# 7

# AN INDIVIDUAL ACCEPTANCE OF RESPONSIBILITY

## INTRODUCTION

Israel's military victories are essential to its survival, but they are not enough. Winning the war is only the first step—winning the peace is the true challenge. Military success can secure borders, but only long-term engagement, education, and advocacy can secure Israel's future in the global arena.

As the world debates Israel's actions, too often the loudest voices are those who have never set foot in the country. Media distortions, ideological bias, and outright falsehoods shape perceptions, turning Israel into a symbol rather than a reality. The 2023 Foundation was founded to change this.

This essay outlines a vision for securing Israel's long-term future—not through abstract diplomacy, but through direct engagement, immersive experiences, and real-world connection. The Foundation's mission is built on the belief that truth cannot be told—it must be experienced. Through scholarships, industry placements, and cultural exchanges, we create opportunities for people to witness Israel's complexity first-hand, breaking through the noise of misinformation.

The stakes could not be higher. If Israel is to thrive beyond the battlefield, it must cultivate a global network of allies who understand, engage, and advocate for the truth. This is not just about Israel—it is about the defence of Western values, the fight against rising antisemitism, and the battle for historical truth.

Victory is not just about surviving. It is about shaping the future.

## A VISION TO HELP "WIN THE PEACE" AFTER ISRAEL WINS THE WAR

*Previously published in The Times of Israel, November 28, 2024, and The Jerusalem Post, December 1, 2024*

"There is nothing more powerful than an idea whose time has come." This phrase, often attributed to Victor Hugo, seems fitting as we contemplate the future of Israel.

With recent military operations in Gaza and Lebanon achieving tactical and strategic successes, and the election of President Trump, Israel is gaining significant ground in its fight for security. Yet, even as the immediate wars are being won, we must look ahead to safeguard Israel's "day after" strategy—a plan critical to securing a lasting peace.

The Government of Israel is, rightly, keeping this plan shielded from those who might exploit it for divisive agendas. However, as an independent advocate for peaceful coexistence, I am free to share my vision for what it takes to "win the peace"—a vision that benefits all those invested in a stable Middle East.

My first career was as a soldier, with thirty years in the Australian Army, serving in conflict zones including Timor-Leste, Bougainville, Iraq, and twice in Afghanistan. From July 2019 to September 2021, I lived in Jerusalem, where I served as a military peacekeeper with the United Nations.

Though I am not Jewish, my experiences there fostered a deep affinity with the Jewish people. The events of October 2023 and the surge of antisemitism that followed strengthened my resolve: I would not be a bystander.

To the Jewish people here and now, I say—you are not alone. There are people "among the nations" with a love for Israel and the Jewish people who will not remain silent in the face of slander, mischaracterisation, and defamation. Antisemitism is a scourge and a rising global challenge.

The 2023 Foundation emerged as a response to this challenge. Our mission is to foster peaceful coexistence and dispel harmful narratives about Israel through immersive, hands-on experiences. We provide scholarships, industry placements, and cultural exchanges to cultivate understanding and empathy. What began in Australia now aims to expand to the US and beyond, building a network of allies united by shared experiences and values.

Our approach is rooted in the belief that "a love for Israel cannot be taught; it must be caught." I came to appreciate Israel by experiencing its landscapes, communities, and complex realities firsthand. The essence of Israel—with all its "perfect imperfections"—can only be understood up close, not through distorted media portrayals.

During my time in Israel, I travelled extensively, often cycling with friends along roads that today bear tragic significance. I remember stopping for coffee in Sderot or Ofakim on some mornings, riding up and down Route 232, now ominously called the "Road of Death."

The tragedy of young lives lost in Re'im, while my daughter was at a similar concert in Sydney, felt deeply personal. This experience, along with others I hold privately, gave me a connection to the grief of my Israeli friends.

In Israel, I witnessed firsthand its pluralistic society—a home for Jews, Christians, Muslims, Druze, and other minorities such as Bahá'í and Circassians. Israel protects the rights of all citizens, regardless of gender, religion, or sexual orientation, yet this reality is rarely conveyed by media dominated by activism and ideological biases. Efforts to address such misrepresentations in casual conversations or on social media often proved futile, met with hostility or outright "cancellation." I realised that a better approach was necessary—one built on real experiences rather than abstract debates.

The 2023 Foundation directly challenges movements like Boycott, Divestment, and Sanctions (BDS), which seek to isolate Israel and deny people the chance to see the country for themselves. BDS severs connections, pushing an agenda of exclusion rather than dialogue. We counter this by promoting engagement—sponsoring trips and internships that reveal Israel's diversity and resilience.

We also take an unapologetic stance on Israel's inclusivity by organising visits, such as for LGBTQ+ communities to Tel Aviv's Pride March. These experiences highlight Israel's vibrant pluralism and refute misconceptions spread by groups like Queers for Palestine, whose paradox is as striking as "Chickens for KFC." Through these initiatives, we aim to cultivate advocates who see beyond stereotypes and appreciate Israel's role as a multicultural democracy.

Our approach draws on the words of Benjamin Franklin: "Tell me, and I forget; teach me, and I may remember; involve me, and I learn."

Participants learn by working alongside Israelis, experiencing the nation's commitment to free-market principles, the rule of law, and social inclusion. They engage with the cooperative spirit driving Israel forward and return with a deep understanding of its unique role in the region.

The Foundation's motto, Facta Non Verba—Deeds, Not Words—guides our actions. We are reclaiming "Zionist" as a proud identity for those who advocate a safe and democratic homeland for the Jewish people. By fostering understanding and supporting Israel's values through real-world interactions, we build allies in the global community.

As we peer past the event horizon of war into the possibilities of peace, the words often attributed to Hugo stated at the beginning resonate with clarity.

The 2023 Foundation's vision is one such idea. If you believe in our mission, if you see value in fostering true understanding and lasting peace, then join us. Together, we can combat antisemitism, promote coexistence, and lift our gaze beyond the immediate challenges. Together, we can help Israel "win the peace" and build a future founded on tolerance, truth, and shared humanity.

# CONCLUSION TO SECTION V

Winning the war is not enough—we must win the peace.

Israel's future cannot be dictated by its enemies or by Western diplomats who do not understand its reality. The Jewish state must shape its own destiny—one built on security, resilience, and an unwavering commitment to truth.

This section has offered a vision for the future, but a vision means nothing without action.

The final chapter of this book will reaffirm what has been made clear throughout these pages: Israel's fight is the fight for civilisation itself. And that fight is far from over.

CONCLUSION

# THE FIGHT FOR CIVILISATION IS NOT OVER

## FACTA NON VERBA—DEEDS, NOT WORDS

History does not move in straight lines. Civilisations rise and fall not because of chance, but because of choices. The choices we make today will determine the fate of Western civilisation, Israel, and the values that have underpinned human progress for centuries.

Throughout this book, we have examined the relentless resurgence of antisemitism, the military and moral struggles of Israel, the war of perception, and the decline of Western clarity and resolve.

But understanding the problem is not enough. Now is the time for action.

We cannot remain silent as antisemitism returns to the mainstream.

We cannot allow lies to replace historical truth.

We cannot let Israel stand alone.

For too long, the Jewish people have been expected to justify their existence, to explain their right to live in their ancestral homeland, and to defend themselves within absurdly constrained limits. Enough.

This book has laid out the moral, strategic, and civilisational stakes of Israel's struggle. But this is not just about Israel. It is about all of us.

## THE STRUGGLE IS FAR FROM OVER

Israel will endure. It always has.

But this is the real question: Will Western civilisation endure with it?

The battle lines have been drawn—not just in Gaza, not just in Jerusalem, but in the lecture halls of universities, the newsrooms of major publications, and the political offices of democratic nations.

There is no neutral ground in this fight. To be silent is to be complicit.

## THE 2023 FOUNDATION – TAKING THE FIGHT BEYOND WORDS

It is one thing to identify the problem. It is another to do something about it.

That is why The 2023 Foundation exists—to combat antisemitism, fight misinformation, and ensure that Israel's story is told with truth and clarity.

- **We will educate**—bringing firsthand experiences to those who have been fed lies.
- **We will advocate**—ensuring that political, media, and academic institutions are held accountable.

- **We will build alliances**—connecting those who understand that Israel's fight is the fight for Western values.

## TOGETHER, WE WILL PREVAIL — חזננ דחי׳

This book is not just a record of what has happened. It is a call to action.

The threats to Israel and Western civilisation are real. But so too is our ability to push back.

Israel does not need to justify its existence. The Jewish people do not need to prove their right to defend themselves. The only question that remains is who will stand with them.

The answer to that question will determine not just the future of Israel but also the future of the world.

Let us choose wisely.

Let us act boldly.

Because the fight for civilisation is not over.

# KEY HISTORICAL EVENTS AND TIMELINE

## INTRODUCTION

The Israeli Palestinian conflict, the global rise of antisemitism, and Israel's role in defending Western civilisation did not emerge in a vacuum. Understanding the historical timeline is essential to cutting through misinformation and distortions.

This appendix provides a concise, fact-based timeline of key events that have shaped Israel's struggle for survival, the resurgence of antisemitism, and the geopolitical reality of the Middle East.

## ANCIENT JEWISH CONNECTION TO THE LAND

The Jewish connection to the Land of Israel is not merely historical—it is foundational, deeply embedded in the fabric of Jewish identity, faith, and nationhood. Long before the rise and fall of empires that sought to dominate the region, the Jewish people had established a sovereign kingdom, with Jerusalem as its spiritual and political heart. Unlike colonial enterprises that sought to conquer and exploit foreign lands, the Jewish presence in Israel was organic, indigenous, and uninterrupted, even through periods of exile. The longing to return to Zion—expressed in prayers, traditions, and scripture—sustained Jewish identity for millennia. From the Babylonian exile to the Roman destruction of the Second Temple, foreign conquests attempted to sever this bond, yet Jewish resilience ensured that Israel remained the eternal homeland of the Jewish people. The renaming of Judea to "Palestina" by the Romans in 135 CE was a deliberate attempt to erase Jewish history, but it failed. The Jewish people never abandoned their claim to the land, and throughout centuries of exile, a continuous Jewish presence remained, standing as a testament to an unbroken connection that no empire or ideology could erase.

- **3761 BCE** – The Jewish Calendar begins, marking the traditional date of Creation according to Jewish tradition.
- **c. 1000 BCE** – King David establishes Jerusalem as the capital of the Jewish people.
- **c. 960 BCE** – King Solomon builds the First Temple in Jerusalem.
- **586 BCE** – The Babylonians destroy the First Temple; Jewish exile begins.
- **515 BCE** – The Second Temple is rebuilt in Jerusalem under Persian rule.
- **70 CE** – The Romans destroy the Second Temple; mass Jewish exile begins (Diaspora).
- **136 CE** – The Bar Kokhba Revolt is crushed; Rome renames Judea to "Palestina" to erase Jewish identity.

**Significance**: The Jewish connection to Israel spans over 3,000 years, long before modern states existed.

## EARLY ISLAMIC AND CHRISTIAN CONTROL OF THE LAND

Throughout history, the Land of Israel remained a focal point of conquest and control by foreign empires, yet Jewish identity and connection to the land never wavered. When Muslim forces took Jerusalem in 636 CE, they imposed Islamic rule but allowed Jewish communities to exist under restrictive conditions. The arrival of the Christian Crusaders in 1099 CE brought another wave of devastation, as both Jews and Muslims were slaughtered in the name of religious conquest. Under the Ottomans (1517–1917), the land remained largely neglected, its population sparse, with Jewish life restricted but never fully extinguished. Despite centuries of foreign rule, Jewish communities persisted in cities like Jerusalem, Hebron, Tiberias, and Safed, maintaining religious, cultural, and historical ties to their ancestral homeland. While others ruled politically, the Jewish people remained spiritually and emotionally bound to Israel, never relinquishing their claim or their longing to return.

- **636 CE** – Muslim forces conquer Jerusalem.
- **1099 CE** – Christian Crusaders capture Jerusalem, massacring Jews and Muslims.
- **1517–1917** – The Ottoman Empire rules the land for 400 years, allowing a limited Jewish presence.

**Significance**: For most of history, Jews were a minority under foreign rule but never relinquished their claim to Israel.

## ZIONISM AND THE ROAD TO STATEHOOD

Zionism, as a spiritual and national longing for the Jewish return to the Land of Israel, dates back to the Babylonian exile (circa 586 BCE), when the First Temple was destroyed, and the Jewish people were forcibly taken to Babylon. During this period, prophets like Jeremiah and Ezekiel, as well as psalmists, expressed the deep yearning to return to Zion (Jerusalem), which became central to Jewish identity and religious practice.

One of the most famous expressions of this longing is found in Psalm 137:5–6 in the King James Version of the Bible:

> "If I forget you, O Jerusalem, let my right
> hand wither.
>
> Let my tongue cleave to the roof of my mouth,
> if I do not remember you,
>
> if I do not set Jerusalem above my highest joy."

This early form of Zionism was religious and spiritual, deeply embedded in Jewish prayers, traditions, and festivals. The longing to return to Israel remained a defining feature of Jewish life throughout centuries of exile.

While the spiritual and cultural form of Zionism dates back over 2,500 years, modern political Zionism emerged in the late nineteenth century, led by figures such as Theodor Herzl (author of *Der Judenstaat*, 1896) and the First Zionist Congress (1897), which formally advocated for the establishment of a Jewish homeland.

- **1897** – The First Zionist Congress, led by Theodor Herzl, calls for a Jewish homeland.
- **1917** – The Balfour Declaration: Britain endorses a Jewish national home in Palestine.

- **1920** – The San Remo Conference: The League of Nations grants Britain a mandate to establish a Jewish homeland.
- **1939** – Britain issues the White Paper, restricting Jewish immigration—even as Jews flee the Holocaust.
- **1947** – The UN Partition Plan proposes separate Jewish and Arab states.
- **Significance:** The Jewish state was not a colonial project but an internationally recognised return to Jewish ancestral land.

## 1948–1973: ISRAEL'S FIGHT FOR SURVIVAL

Between 1948 and 1973, Israel's survival was anything but guaranteed. From the moment it declared independence, the fledgling state was thrust into a relentless struggle for existence, facing existential threats from hostile neighbours determined to erase it from the map. Each war Israel fought during this period was not a matter of territorial ambition but of sheer necessity—wars of survival against overwhelming odds. The international community often framed these conflicts in terms of diplomacy and ceasefires, but for Israel, they were battles for its very right to exist.

Despite being outnumbered and outgunned, Israel demonstrated extraordinary military ingenuity and resilience, achieving stunning victories in conflicts like the Six-Day War of 1967, where it not only repelled its adversaries but also reunited Jerusalem and secured strategically vital territories. However, these victories came at great cost, as seen in the Yom Kippur War of 1973, when Israel faced a surprise attack on the holiest day of the Jewish calendar, pushing its defences to the brink before ultimately prevailing.

These wars shaped Israel's national psyche and reinforced a core lesson: Security could never be outsourced or taken for granted. Every concession, every ceasefire, and every diplomatic negotiation had to be weighed against the harsh reality that Israel's enemies did not seek peace but rather its annihilation. Survival was not a right—it was something that had to be defended with unrelenting vigilance.

- **May 14, 1948** – Israel declares independence.
- **May 15, 1948** – Five Arab armies invade Israel; the War of Independence begins.
- **1949** – An armistice is signed, but no peace follows; Israel's borders remain under threat.
- **1956 – Suez Crisis:** Egypt blocks Israeli shipping; Israel captures Sinai but later withdraws under US pressure.
- **1967 – Six-Day War:** Israel defeats Egypt, Jordan, and Syria, regaining Jerusalem, Judea and Samaria (West Bank), Gaza, Sinai, and the Golan Heights.
- **1973 – Yom Kippur War:** Israel survives a surprise attack by Egypt and Syria but at a high cost.

**Significance**: Israel's wars were defensive; Arab states repeatedly sought Israel's destruction.


## PEACE EFFORTS AND TERRORISM

Israel's repeated efforts to achieve peace have been met with cycles of rejection, terrorism, and violence. The 1979 Camp David Accords demonstrated Israel's willingness to make historic concessions, including returning the Sinai Peninsula to

Egypt, in exchange for peace. Similarly, the 1993 Oslo Accords saw Israel recognise the Palestinian Authority (PA) and grant it governance over parts of the West Bank and Gaza, with the hope of establishing lasting peace. However, these overtures were not reciprocated. Instead of fostering stability, the 2000 Second Intifada erupted, unleashing a wave of suicide bombings and terrorist attacks that claimed over 1,000 Israeli lives. The 2005 Gaza Disengagement, in which Israel withdrew all its citizens and military from Gaza, was intended to pave the way for Palestinian self-rule and economic development. Instead, Hamas seized control of Gaza in 2007 and transformed the region into a launching pad for thousands of rocket attacks on Israeli civilians. Each of these events underscores a painful reality: Israel has repeatedly taken risks for peace, but Palestinian leadership and terrorist factions have consistently responded with violence and rejectionism, undermining every opportunity for coexistence.

- **1979 – Camp David Accords:** Israel and Egypt sign a peace treaty.
- **1993 – Oslo Accords:** The PA is established; Israel grants autonomy to Palestinians.
- **2000 – Second Intifada:** Palestinian terrorists launch a wave of suicide bombings, killing over 1,000 Israelis.
- **2005 – Gaza Disengagement:** Israel withdraws from Gaza unilaterally; Hamas takes control in 2007.

**Significance:** Israel has repeatedly sought peace, but Palestinian leadership has rejected or undermined opportunities.

## MODERN CHALLENGES: 2008–PRESENT

Since 2008, Israel has faced relentless attacks from Hamas and other terrorist groups, leading to multiple military operations aimed at restoring deterrence. Despite repeated ceasefires and diplomatic efforts, Hamas has continued to fire rockets indiscriminately at Israeli civilians, using Gaza as a base for terror. However, there have also been significant diplomatic breakthroughs, most notably the 2020 Abraham Accords, which saw Israel establish historic peace agreements with the United Arab Emirates, Bahrain, Morocco, and Sudan, proving that regional cooperation is possible when leaders prioritise stability over hostility.

This fragile balance was shattered on October 7, 2023, when Hamas launched the deadliest terrorist attack in Israel's history, murdering over 1,200 men, women, and children, committing atrocities that shocked the world. The next day, Hezbollah intensified hostilities, launching rockets and conducting cross-border raids from Lebanon, escalating the conflict into a multi-front war. In response, Israel launched a full-scale military operation to dismantle Hamas's terrorist infrastructure in Gaza, while simultaneously reinforcing its northern borders against Hezbollah's aggression.

The repercussions have been global. Antisemitism has surged worldwide, fuelled by misinformation, ideological extremism, and media distortions that seek to demonise Israel's right to self-defence. Israel remains on the front line in the fight against terrorism and the broader battle to uphold Western democratic values. As the conflict continues, one question remains: Will the world finally acknowledge the reality of Israel's struggle, or will history repeat itself once again?

- **2008–2023** – Multiple wars are waged with Hamas, as rocket attacks on Israeli civilians continue.
- **2020** – **Abraham Accords:** Israel normalises relations with the UAE, Bahrain, Morocco, and Sudan.
- **October 7, 2023** – Hamas launches the largest terror attack in Israel's history; over 1,200 murdered.
- **October 8, 2023** – Hezbollah launches rocket and drone attacks.
- **Present** – Antisemitism surges worldwide.

**Significance**: The fight against terrorism and antisemitism is ongoing, with Israel remaining on the front line of Western values.

APPENDIX B

# INTERNATIONAL LAW AND THE ETHICS OF WARFARE

## INTRODUCTION

Israel is held to a unique and often impossible standard in warfare. While other nations engage in conflicts with little scrutiny, Israel faces relentless accusations of war crimes, disproportionate force, and violations of international law—even when acting in self-defence.

This appendix outlines the key principles of international law, the ethics of warfare, and how Israel adheres to some of the strictest military codes in the world.

## THE FOUNDATIONS OF INTERNATIONAL LAW IN ARMED CONFLICT

Modern warfare is governed by a series of international treaties and legal principles, the most significant of which include the following:

- **The Hague Conventions (1899, 1907)** – Established the first rules on warfare, including the prohibition of unnecessary suffering
- **The Geneva Conventions (1949, Additional Protocols in 1977)** – Set the legal framework for protecting civilians, prisoners of war, and combatants in armed conflicts
- **UN Charter (1945)** – Establishes the right of nations to self-defence under Article 51
- **Rome Statute of the International Criminal Court (ICC) (1998)** – Defines war crimes, genocide, and crimes against humanity

**Significance**: These laws form the basis of just war theory—ensuring military actions are conducted with moral and legal legitimacy.

## THE PRINCIPLE OF SELF-DEFENCE UNDER INTERNATIONAL LAW

Israel's military actions are guided by Article 51 of the UN Charter, which affirms a nation's right to self-defence.

- **The 1948 Arab-Israeli War** – Israel was invaded the day after its independence.
- **The 1967 Six-Day War** – It began when Israel launched a pre-emptive strike after months of escalating Arab military threats, including the massing of Egyptian, Syrian, and Jordanian troops along its borders. The situation intensified when Egypt expelled UN peacekeepers from the Sinai Peninsula and imposed a naval blockade on the Straits of Tiran—a critical shipping route for Israeli trade, particularly oil. This, along with

hostile rhetoric and defence pacts among Arab states, made war seem imminent. Israel acted decisively to protect its national security against an existential threat.

- **The Yom Kippur War (1973)** – Israel defended itself from a surprise attack by Egypt and Syria.
- **Gaza Conflicts (2008, 2012, 2014, 2021, 2023)** – All of these conflicts were responses to Hamas rocket attacks on Israeli civilians.

**Significance**: Under international law, Israel is fully entitled to respond with force when its citizens are under attack.

## PROPORTIONALITY AND DISCRIMINATION IN WARFARE

Two key principles of just war theory apply to all military engagements:

- **Proportionality** – The military response must be proportional to the threat.
- **Discrimination** – Combatants must distinguish between military targets and civilians.

## HOW ISRAEL COMPLIES:

- **Warning Civilians Before Strikes** – Israel declares active military zones foregoing the element of surprise, drops leaflets, makes phone calls, uses loud hailers broadcast in Arabic, and uses the "knock on the roof" tactic to warn civilians before airstrikes.
- **Surgical Precision** – Israel uses intelligence and precision munitions to target terrorists, not civilians.

- **Field Hospitals for Enemies** – The Israel Defense Forces (IDF) has treated Palestinian civilians and even wounded terrorists.

## HOW HAMAS VIOLATES THESE LAWS:

- **Rocket Attacks on Civilians** – Hamas deliberately targets Israeli cities.
- **Human Shields** – Hamas embeds its fighters in hospitals, schools, and mosques.
- **Misinformation Warfare** – Civilian casualty figures are fabricated to manipulate global opinion.

**Significance**: Israel follows higher ethical standards than any military in the world, despite fighting an enemy that flagrantly violates international law.

## DOUBLE STANDARDS IN GLOBAL WARFARE ACCOUNTABILITY

Israel is singled out for scrutiny, while other nations operate without consequence:

- **Russia's Invasion of Ukraine** – Despite mass war crimes, Russia faces fewer UN investigations than Israel.
- **China's Genocide of Uyghurs** – There have been no UN Human Rights Council resolutions condemning China's actions.

**Significance**: No other country is expected to fight wars with zero casualties or justify every defensive action the way Israel is.

## THE LEGALITY OF ISRAELI SETTLEMENTS AND TERRITORIAL DISPUTES

There is a common misconception that Israeli settlements violate international law. Here are the facts:

- **UN Resolution 242 (1967)** – Does not require Israel to return all territories captured in 1967
- **League of Nations Mandate (1922)** – Recognises the Jewish right to settle in Judea and Samaria (West Bank)
- **Territorial Status Before 1967** – Confirms no prior Palestinian sovereignty, as the West Bank was Jordanian and Gaza was Egyptian

**Significance**: The legal status of Israeli settlements is disputed, not illegal, and past peace agreements have acknowledged that final borders require negotiation.

## HAMAS, WAR CRIMES, AND THE ETHICS OF ASYMMETRICAL WARFARE

Hamas violates every principle of international law:

- Deliberate attacks on civilians (more than 15,000 rockets fired at Israeli cities)
- Use of human shields (placing military sites in civilian areas)
- Kidnapping and hostage-taking (October 7, 2023)
- Execution of suspected collaborators without trial

**Significance**: Israel's war is not a conventional state-to-state conflict but a fight against an enemy that uses civilians as pawns and rejects all norms of warfare.

Israel has one of the most legally and ethically restrained militaries in history. It fights against a lawless terrorist entity while being held to standards no other nation faces.

# RESOURCES FOR FURTHER READING AND ENGAGEMENT

## INTRODUCTION

Understanding Israel's struggle, the rise of antisemitism, and the broader defence of Western civilisation requires ongoing education, engagement, and activism.

This appendix provides recommended books, articles, websites, organisations, and media sources to deepen your knowledge and offer ways to get involved.

## ESSENTIAL BOOKS ON ISRAEL, ANTISEMITISM, AND GEOPOLITICS

For those looking to understand Israel's history, security challenges, and the broader ideological battle, these books are essential reading:

### History of Israel and Zionism

*Israel: A Concise History of a Nation Reborn* – Daniel Gordis
*My Promised Land: The Triumph and Tragedy of Israel* – Ari Shavit

*The Case for Israel* – Alan Dershowitz
*Six Days of War* – Michael B. Oren (on the 1967 war)

## Understanding Antisemitism

*Antisemitism: Here and Now* – Deborah E. Lipstadt
*Jews Don't Count* – David Baddiel
*People Love Dead Jews* – Dara Horn

## Terrorism, Security, and Global Threats

*Son of Hamas* – Mosab Hassan Yousef (a Hamas insider's story)
*Rise and Kill First: The Secret History of Israel's Targeted Assassinations* – Ronen Bergman
*Defeating Jihad* – Dr. Sebastian Gorka

## The Battle for Western Civilisation

*The Strange Death of Europe* – Douglas Murray
*The War of Return* – Adi Schwartz and Einat Wilf
*The Fate of the West* – Bill Emmott

**Significance**: These books offer factual, well-researched insights to counter misinformation and historical distortions.

# RECOMMENDED ARTICLES AND REPORTS

For those seeking deep-dive analysis and policy insights, the following reports and articles provide fact-based perspectives on Israel, antisemitism, and security threats:

*The Hamas Covenant* (1988, 2017 update) – Official document revealing Hamas's genocidal intent.

*The ADL's Annual Report on Global Antisemitism* – Tracks worldwide antisemitic incidents.

The Jerusalem Center for Public Affairs (JCPA) Security Reports – Analysis of Israel's strategic challenges.

FDD (Foundation for Defense of Democracies) Reports – Covers Iran's nuclear threat and Middle East security issues.

**Significance**: These reports offer data-driven perspectives on security, terrorism, and antisemitism.

## RELIABLE WEBSITES AND NEWS SOURCES

Israel and the Middle East are often misrepresented in mainstream media. The following sources provide accurate reporting and expert analysis:

### News and Analysis

*The Times of Israel* – Balanced reporting on Israel and Jewish affairs.

*The Jerusalem Post* – English-language coverage of Israeli and Middle Eastern news.

*Tablet* – In-depth essays on Jewish identity, Israel, and culture.

### Think Tanks and Policy Institutes

Middle East Media Research Institute (MEMRI) – Translates Arab, Persian, and Turkish media.

Begin–Sadat Center for Strategic Studies (BESA) – Israeli security and defence research.

The Institute for National Security Studies (INSS) – Analysis of Israel's military and geopolitical landscape.

CAMERA (Committee for Accuracy in Middle East Reporting and Analysis) – Challenges anti-Israel media bias.

**Significance:** These sources provide credible information that counteracts media distortions and ideological bias.

## ORGANISATIONS FIGHTING ANTISEMITISM AND SUPPORTING ISRAEL

Many activist groups and educational organisations work to expose antisemitism and defend Israel in political, media, and academic circles.

### Fighting Antisemitism: Key Organisations

The 2023 Foundation – An organisation dedicated to combating antisemitism and fostering peaceful coexistence.

The Dor Foundation – An Australian not-for-profit, non-partisan organisation established to combat antisemitism and hate. Chaired by former Federal Treasurer Josh Frydenberg, it focuses on building tolerance and social cohesion, particularly on university campuses and online platforms.

Combat Antisemitism Movement (CAM) – A global coalition uniting organisations and individuals to fight antisemitism through policy initiatives, education, and advocacy.

Never Again Is Now (NAIN) – A movement dedicated to ensuring the lessons of history are applied today to prevent the resurgence of antisemitism.

Anti-Defamation League (ADL) – One of the world's oldest and most recognised organisations, committed to tracking, exposing, and confronting antisemitism and hate speech.

StandWithUs – A non-partisan educational organisation focused on advocating for Israel and countering misinformation in media, academia, and public discourse.

Foundation to Combat Antisemitism (FCAS) – Led by philanthropist Robert Kraft, this foundation actively supports education and action-based programmes to fight antisemitism and promote Jewish identity.

**Significance**: These organisations work tirelessly to expose antisemitism, challenge misinformation, and ensure the safety and dignity of Jewish communities worldwide.

## SUPPORTING ISRAEL IN POLITICS AND MEDIA

HonestReporting – A media watchdog organisation that monitors, exposes, and corrects bias against Israel in mainstream reporting.

UN Watch – A Geneva-based watchdog organisation that monitors the United Nations for bias, hypocrisy, and double standards, particularly regarding Israel. It exposes UN agencies that single out Israel unfairly while ignoring human rights abuses worldwide and advocates for accountability within international institutions.

The American Jewish Committee (AJC) – A leading organisation committed to defending Jewish communities, combating antisemitism, and advocating for Israel on the global stage.

Sky News Australia – A prominent news outlet that challenges mainstream narratives, providing critical analysis and perspectives on Israel and global politics.

The Daily Wire – A conservative media organisation known for its strong advocacy of Western values, free speech, and factual reporting on Israel and Middle East affairs.

The Free Press – An independent news platform dedicated to truthful journalism and countering misinformation, particularly regarding Israel and global conflicts.

**Significance**: These organisations and media platforms play a vital role in shaping public perception, correcting misinformation, and advocating for Israel's right to self-defence.

## HOW TO ENGAGE AND TAKE ACTION

Understanding the issues is only the first step—here's how you can actively support Israel and combat antisemitism:

- **Challenge misinformation online** – Correct anti-Israel falsehoods on social media.
- **Join or support an Israel advocacy group** – Many organisations need volunteers and donations.
- **Write to politicians** – Demand that they support Israel's right to self-defence.
- **Educate your community** – Share factual sources with friends and family.
- **Visit Israel** – Seeing the reality firsthand is the best way to counter propaganda.

**Significance**: The fight for truth, justice, and Israel's future requires real-world engagement, not just passive support.

The battle for Israel's legitimacy and the defence of Western values is fought through knowledge, courage, and one conversation at a time.

# ABOUT THE 2023 FOUNDATION AND HOW TO SUPPORT IT

## OUR MISSION: COMBATING ANTISEMITISM THROUGH EDUCATION AND ENGAGEMENT

The 2023 Foundation is an Australian non-profit organisation committed to combating antisemitism and strengthening relationships with Israel. We achieve this by incentivising educational visits to Israel, offering scholarships, and creating opportunities that foster a deep understanding of Israel's unique contributions to the world.

## EDUCATIONAL INITIATIVES: BRIDGING GAPS THROUGH FIRSTHAND EXPERIENCE

Recognising that Israel is often misunderstood due to persistent misinformation, we tackle these misconceptions by offering grounded perspectives and fostering unfiltered engagement. Our educational programmes enable participants to experience the true reality of Israel's achievements and challenges, promoting a more informed and nuanced understanding.

## THEMATIC VISITS: IMMERSIVE JOURNEYS TO THE HEART OF ISRAEL

We organise thematic group visits to Israel for diverse participants, including veterans and students. These immersive journeys allow individuals to engage directly with Israel's culture, history, and people, fostering personal connections and dispelling myths perpetuated by biased narratives.

## SCHOLARSHIPS AND PLACEMENTS: INVESTING IN FUTURE AMBASSADORS

To further our mission, we offer financial support through scholarships and facilitate vocational placements related to Israel. By empowering individuals to pursue educational and professional opportunities, we cultivate a network of informed ambassadors committed to promoting understanding and combating antisemitism in their respective communities.

## ALUMNI NETWORK: SUSTAINING IMPACT THROUGH CONTINUED ENGAGEMENT

Our commitment extends beyond initial programmes; we maintain an active alumni network that encourages participants to share their experiences and insights. This community fosters ongoing dialogue and collaboration, creating a ripple effect of understanding and advocacy that amplifies our impact globally.

## ORIGINS AND LEADERSHIP: A PERSONAL COMMITMENT TO CHANGE

My wife, Dracaena, and I lived in Israel from 2019 to 2021. The 2023 Foundation was born out of our deep personal connection to the land and its people. The events of October 7, 2023, and the subsequent rise in antisemitism worldwide, particularly in Australia, compelled us to act. Leveraging a lifetime of professional experience, we established the Foundation to make a meaningful difference and build a legacy of understanding and tolerance.

For more information, please visit our website at www.2023foundation.org.au.

# ACKNOWLEDGMENTS

Grant McCorquodale
Rabbi Raffi Kaiserblueth
Dr. Ron Weiser, AM
Cedric Geffen
Carol Tannous Sleiman
Avi Cohen
Elad Gur
Judi Hall
Kati Haworth
Gareth Narunsky
Sharonne Philips
Yvonne and Bobby Steinberg
the late Judith Kaye
the late Paul Keen
Yossi Eshed
Shai and Talila Lachman
Keren Preiskel
Carolyn and Tony Ziegler
David and Caroline Lewis
Laura Taitz
Richard and Nancy Perl
Justine Pogroske
Owen Nathan
Peter Philippsohn, OAM

Alana Kennedy and
   Michael Hendler
Michael and Mary Easson
Linda Royal
Yaron Finkelstein
Jake Wallis Simons
Ali Tabrizi
Joel Burnie
Jacqui Bakker
Sarah Way
Maxime and Jim Carlil
Peter Werteim
Tali Shine
Mark Leach
Ben Klein
Sam Babus
Lynda Ben-Menashe
Esther Kubie
Yoav Tourel
Alex Ryvchin
Roland Gridiger
David Shein
Dean Blomson
Melissa and Barry McCurdie

Peter Lerner
Daniel Berke
Paul Israel
Fatima Rozenblit
Marnie Pernstein
Nathan Joel
Noa Sheer
Jacob Smit
Norma Barne
Judy Swan
Kelly Bayer Rosmarin
Kevin Kalinko
Daniel Greengarten
Vladimir Bermant
Dr. Michael Oren

Ido Aharoni
Shelly Freeman
Patrick Mayoh
Marcia and Bernie Kresner
Chloe and Lance Cohen
Frieda Kahn
John Roth
Stanley Roth
Rivka Kidron
Alethea Gold
Daniel Lipshut
Shoshana and Jason Eisner
The Australian Jewish News
The Times of Israel
The Jerusalem Post

# ABOUT THE AUTHOR

Michael is Founder of the 2023 Foundation, a charity to combat antisemitism. He is a veteran of the Australian Army who commemorated thirty years of full-time service in March 2024. His operational experience includes deployments to Timor-Leste, Bougainville, Iraq, and two tours of Afghanistan.

From July 2019 to September 2021, Michael was seconded to the United Nations in the Middle East. He served as Head of Military, United Nations Truce Supervision Organisation, and resided in Jerusalem with his wife, Dracaena.

During this time, his mission area covered Israel, Lebanon, Syria, Jordan, and Egypt, where he travelled extensively, gaining remarkable insights. For his service on this mission, Michael was awarded the Conspicuous Service Cross by the

Governor-General of Australia in the 2023 Australia Day Honours List.

Michael is a graduate of Duntroon and holds a Bachelor of Management from Southern Cross University, a Master of Management, and a Master of Arts from the University of New South Wales. In 2024, he was awarded a scholarship and is completing a full-time Master of Business Administration (MBA) at the Australian Graduate School of Management. As part of his MBA, Michael studied on exchange at New York University's Stern School of Business.

The events of October 7, 2023, and the October 9, 2023, protest at the Opera House, along with the aftermath, deeply impacted Michael. In July 2024, he founded The 2023 Foundation Ltd, a company dedicated to combating antisemitism. Michael is determined not to be a bystander and is motivated to partner and collaborate with those who share his passion and purpose. Together, we will prevail! חצנב דחי

Although Michael is not Jewish, he has a deep affinity and abiding respect for the Jewish people. In October 2024, he was made an honorary Life Member of Emanuel Synagogue in Woollahra, Sydney. Having witnessed firsthand Israel's remarkable story, Michael is dedicated to ensuring that this story is both seen and heard.